LARGE FAMILIES
IN LONDON

(A Study of 86 Families)

HILARY LAND

Department of Social Administration
London School of Economics
and Political Science

OCCASIONAL PAPERS ON SOCIAL ADMINISTRATION NO. 32
Editorial Committee under the Chairmanship of Professor R. M. Titmuss

Published by G. Bell & Sons Ltd.
York House, Portugal Street, London, W.C.2

First Published 1969
© *Copyright 1969 by The Social Administration Research Trust*

SBN 7135 1577 5

MADE AND PRINTED IN GREAT BRITAIN BY
WILLMER BROTHERS LIMITED
BIRKENHEAD

This series of *Occasional Papers* was started in 1960 to supply the need for a medium of publication for studies in the field of social policy and administration which fell between the two extremes of the short article and the full-length book. It was thought that such a series would not only meet a need among research workers and writers concerned with contemporary social issues, but would also strengthen the links between students of the subject and administrators, social workers, committee members and others with responsibilities and interest in the social services.

Contributions to the series should be submitted to the Editorial Committee. A list of earlier papers in this series which are still in print is to be found on the back of this volume.

Richard M. Titmuss

CONTENTS

This pilot study is one of a series[1] carried out in association with a national survey whose aims are to define poverty in terms relevant for the present day and to measure its overall incidence. The field work was completed three and a half years ago. No account has been taken of any changes in benefit rates, school meal provisions or other social services since the fieldwork was undertaken, although they are discussed in the concluding Chapter.

The poverty research team was assisted by an Advisory Committee whose members were Professor R. M. Titmuss (London School of Economics), Mr. Ford Longman (Joseph Rowntree Memorial Trust), Professor D. C. Marsh (University of Nottingham), Mr. Leonard Nicholson (Central Statistical Office), Miss Jean Rowntree (Joseph Rowntree Memorial Trust), Sir Donald Sargent (Supplementary Bene-fits Commission), Mr. Lewis Waddilove (Joseph Rowntree Memorial Trust) and Professor J. Yudkin (Queen Elizabeth College, University of London), all of whom served in a personal capacity.

I should like to thank the Joseph Rowntree Memorial Trustees for their generous financial support and members of the Advisory Com-mittee for their help in preparing the plans for this study. None of them, of course, is responsible for any of the methods adopted or for any of the views expressed in this report.

I am indebted to Brian Abel-Smith and Peter Townsend who first encouraged me to study large families. Without their advice, help and criticism at every stage of the study this report would never have been written. I also owe much to the numerous discussions with the other members of the poverty research team. John Veit Wilson helped me particularly in the early stages of this study and Dennis Marsden and Adrian Sinfield read my drafts at every stage, providing much tough but valuable comment. Sheila Benson and Marie Brown have also read preliminary drafts.

The staff of the Ministry of Pensions and National Insurance gave

---

1. The other studies are *Mothers Alone* by Dennis Marsden, Allen Lane the Penguin Press 1969, *Unemployed in Shields* by Adrian Sinfield (to be published) and a study of the chronic sick by John Veit Wilson.

their time in providing me with a sample of families. Later I received useful advice and criticism on the final drafts from officials of the Ministry of Social Security. I have tried to take account of their comments, but of course I remain responsible for all that is written here.

At other times I have received advice or comments on my drafts from Judy Bernstein, Bob Deacon, Tony Lynes, Ruth Michaels, Mike Miller, Garth Plowman, Martin Rein, Hilary Rose and Sally Sainsbury.

I am very grateful to Bridget Atkinson and June Hillage for their help in preparing typed drafts from my scripts.

Finally I would like to thank the mothers and the fathers of the large families who gave so much of their time patiently answering my questions. My main debt, is, of course, to them.

November 1969

1. INTRODUCTION

This is a study in depth of the living standards of eighty-six London families with five or more dependent children.[1] The fieldwork was undertaken between February 1965 and April 1966. In June 1966, the Ministry of Pensions and National Insurance,[2] in co-operation with the National Assistance Board carried out a national survey of the circumstances of families with two or more children. This study may be regarded as complementing the findings of that survey.[3]

At the turn of the century the majority of families were large.[4] Now only a small minority of completed families have more than four children. The proportion of families with four or more children after decreasing for several decades has been increasing again recently.[5] In 1966 there were about 250,000 families in Britain with five or more children and there were about 1,450,000 children in such families.[6] Moreover, the proportion of children who at some time find themselves members of a family of five or more is considerable, and is under-estimated in statistics referring to incomplete as well as complete families. For example in a survey of twenty-

---

1. Dependent children were defined as children under sixteen years old or still at school. It also included children who were not resident at home but for whose maintenance parents were contributing at least £3 per week.

2. The functions of the Ministry of Pensions and National Insurance were taken over by the Ministry of Social Security created under the Social Security Act 1966 in the Autumn of 1966. The National Assistance Board was subsumed under the new Ministry as the Supplementary Benefits Commission. Since Autumn 1968 the functions of the Ministry of Social Security and the Ministry of Health have been amalgamated in the Department of Health and Social Security. All the information in this study comes from the period before these changes, and reference will therefore be made to 'national assistance' and the National Assistance Board rather than the current terms which are 'supplementary benefits' and the "Supplementary Benefits Commission".
   The scales of payment current at the time of the survey have been used throughout the report.

3. The Ministry's survey provides a statistical framework about the incomes and sources of incomes of families. Full information was given by 2,409 families, or 90 per cent of the original sample. Ministry of Social Security, *Circumstances of Families*, London, H.M.S.O., 1967.

4. Evidence from 1911 on Families with 5 + children. Fertility Census, England and Wales, 1911.

5. For example, between 1953 and 1965 the number of fifth and sixth children in families for whom family allowances were being paid increased by 63 per cent and 84 per cent respectively, although the total number of children for whom allowances were being paid increased by only 25 per cent. *Report of the Ministry of Pensions and National Insurance for the year 1953*, Cmd. 9159, London, H.M.S.O. 1954. *Report of the Ministry of Pensions and National Insurance for the year 1965*. Cmnd. 3046. London, H.M.S.O., 1966.

6. *Circumstances of Families, loc. cit.*, figures in Tables A.1 and A.3 adjusted to conform with total number of families as given on p. 8. See also Central Statistical Office, *Annual Abstract of Statistics*, p. 53.

one year olds born in 1940–41 the Robbins Committee found that 23 per cent had come from a family of five or more children.[7]

Inevitably large families suffer economic disadvantage, because more children have to be supported out of one wage or salary. Moreover the care of a large family limits the ability of the mother to take on paid employment.

Over the past five or six years, evidence has been accumulated which quantifies the disadvantages of members of large families compared with the general population. Royston Lambert, for example, showed that the proportion of children in families with three or more children which were on average deficient in at least two nutrients had actually increased between 1955 and 1960, and also pointed out: 'Large families constitute one of the biggest groups, along with the aged, among those in poverty in Britain. There is evidence that the financial burden of a large family has increased over the decade and that the nutritional position of those groups suffered as a result of decontrol in the middle-fifties.'[8] There was evidence of consequential differences in height and weight: 'There is a slight, but definite, tendency for the less able pupils to be smaller and weigh less than the brighter pupils—the puny looking child as it turns out, is not so likely to be the studious bookworm. It may well be that there is a comparable development in physical and in mental growth in the years of adolescence—a good deal of medical research suggests that there is, but it is also notable that the less successful children tend to come from the larger families (this is true irrespective of social class or background), and there is some evidence that children in small families tend to be taller and heavier.'[9]

Evidence on the educational handicaps of children from large families, based on a continuing survey of a national sample of children born in March 1946, has been presented by J. W. B. Douglas. He found that the average level of mental ability declines with each increase in family size and in the ten years between 1947 and 1957, the relation between the mental ability of an eleven year old and the size of his family had remained substantially unchanged. Children from large families were found to be a little more handicapped in reading, arithmetic and the understanding of words, than in tests of non-verbal intelligence.[10] He goes on to say that this finding cannot be explained entirely in terms of hereditary: that only the poorer, less intelligent parents have large families, because Douglas found that in every social class family size had an

7. *Higher Education*, (The Robbins Report) Appendix One, Cmd. 2154–1, London, H.M.S.O., pp. 61–62.
8. Lambert R., *Nutrition in Britain*, 1950–60, Occasional Papers on Social Administration, No. 6, London, Bell, 1964, p. 46.
9. Ministry of Education, *Half Our Future*, A Report of the Central Advisory Council for Education (England), London, H.M.S.O., 1963, p. 11.
10. Douglas, J. W. B., *The Home and the School*, London, MacGibbon & Kee, 1964, Chapter 10, pp. 92–93.

influence on intelligence. Furthermore, the Robbins Committee found that a child from a family of one or two children was more than twice as likely as a child from a family of five or more children to reach higher education. This remained true whatever the education of the parents.[11] Studies of peri-natal mortality,[12] and homelessness[13] also indicate the disadvantages of large families.

Secondary analysis of the Family Expenditure Survey showed that in 1960 more large than small families were living below or only just above the National Assistance level of living.[14] This has been confirmed by the Ministry of Social Security's recent survey of families.[15] But what do such statements mean in terms of the standards of everyday life? How do parents manage and what do they feel about their problems? How far do the disadvantages of low income correspond with the disadvantages of poor housing and schooling? Are handicaps more a reflection of the size of the family or mainly a reflection of the fact that large families are more often found in the lower income groups? Furthermore, why does a couple have a large family? Are couples who do, different from the rest of the population and are they made to feel different? The attitudes of the community towards a minority group can restrict the lives of its members considerably and may increase their problems.

The purpose of studying a small sample of large families drawn from all income groups was to enable some of these questions to be answered and thus to explore the scale and causes of and the attitudes towards poverty among such families.

The Sample

Every family with at least two dependent children is entitled to a family allowance for the second and any subsequent child.[16] The Ministry of Social Security has a record of every family to whom family allowances are being paid, together with the number of dependent children in that family. Very few families with more than four children fail to collect their family allowances, so the Ministry possesses a virtually complete list of large families in England and Wales.[17] The Ministry agreed to use these records to obtain a

---

11. *Higher Education*, Appendix One, *op. cit.*, p. 61.
12. Butler, N. R. and Bonham, D. G., *Peri-natal Mortality:* the first report of the 1958 British Peri-natal Mortality Survey, Under the Auspices of the National Birthday Trust Fund, Edinburgh, Livingstone, 1963.
13. Greve, J., *London's Homeless*, Occasional Papers on Social Administration, No. 10, London, Bell, 1965.
14. Twenty-five per cent of households with six or more members, compared with between 6 and 7 per cent of households with three or four members, had low incomes. Abel-Smith, B. and Townsend, P., *The Poor and the Poorest*, Occasional Papers on Social Administration, No. 17, London, Bell, 1965, p. 40.
15. Among families with fathers in full-time work 14 per cent of those with six or more children and 7 per cent of those with five children, compared with one per cent of those with two children, had resources below requirements, as measured by basic national assistance scales. Ministry of Social Security , *Circumstances of Families*, *op. cit.*, p. 21.
16. For family allowances purposes, a person is treated as a child while under the upper limit of compulsory education, or during any period before attaining the age of nineteen years while undergoing full-time instruction in a school or while an apprentice earning not more than £2 a week.
17. For a discussion of the method of sampling see Appendix I.

random sample of 150 large families living throughout the London postal district. The sample was chosen so as to give equal numbers of families with five, six or seven children and rather fewer with eight or more. London was chosen to confine the sample to a densely populated, easily accessible area.[18] As a result there may be some characteristics of the families in this study which are peculiar to London, for example, a relatively higher proportion who are immigrant families and who have housing difficulties.

For reasons of confidentiality the Ministry could not disclose to us the name or address of any family before it was contacted. Therefore each family in the sample was sent a letter by the Ministry.[19] Out of the 150 families contacted in this way only thirty-five replied and of those all but one were interviewed during the spring of 1965. In the autumn of that year the Ministry agreed to send a reminder letter, and fifty-two of the 100 families still living at the same address were subsequently interviewed between October 1965 and March 1966. Altogether eight-six families containing 617 children were interviewed, so the final response rate was 57 per cent.

The response rate was by no means as high as we should have liked it to be, but considering that the initial approach had been made indirectly by post and that some months had elapsed between the first and second postal contact the response is not unsatisfactory.[20] In fact, relatively more of the larger than of the smaller families responded positively. Rather less than half the parents of five children but over four-fifths of the parents of eight children were eventually interviewed. In a number of respects the sample resembled the large families included in the Ministry's 1966 survey throughout Britain. For example, the proportions of fathers in full-time work, of mothers earning and of families with resources below requirements were very similar.

The data from this small sample[21] does not allow us to measure the incidence of different phenomena but it does provide descriptive evidence of the characteristics and problems of large families. In particular it indicates which problems are eased, if not completely solved, where the family's income is higher than average.

The Interview

The bulk of the information was collected from the mother, who was interviewed in most instances before the father. This interview

---

18. Less than 2 per cent of households contain five or more dependent children.
19. The letter is shown in Appendix I.
20. The response rate in postal surveys, even after several approaches, often falls short of two-thirds. In income and expenditure surveys, even when there is a financial incentive to give an interview and keep an account of expenditure, the response rarely exceeds 75 per cent. For example, the response rate in The Department of Employment and Productivity's Family Expenditure Survey is just over 70 per cent
21. In the tables throughout this report percentages with a base less than 50 are put in brackets to remind the reader that they should be interpreted with caution.

took on average one and a half hours, though it could take as long as four hours depending on the size of the family and its problems and the number of distractions provided by the children. Although the interview took place whenever possible in school hours, there could be three toddlers present claiming their mother's attention. Most of the mothers were very willing to talk. Perhaps this was because their lives were so absorbed with cooking, cleaning, washing, and shopping for several children, as well as in some cases earning money to help support them, that they were glad of the excuse to sit down and just talk for an hour or so. Details of the father's income were obtained from the father himself in an interview which usually took place subsequently and lasted between half an hour and an hour. He was usually interviewed in the presence of his wife and some of the children, though wives were so often busy or distracted at the time by the children that opportunities were taken to ask husbands 'privately' about earnings. It is possible nonetheless that in a minority of instances earnings may have been understated. Altogether seventy of the eighty-six fathers were interviewed. Two families were fatherless. In another fourteen families he was unwilling to be interviewed. In these instances some information on his earnings was obtained from the mother. (In six families there was insufficient information to calculate the family's income.) Information collected during both interviews was recorded on the questionnaire and this was supplemented by reports on each family written very shortly afterwards.

After obtaining permission from the Inner London Education Authority and the other Education Authorities involved, additional material on each of the 398 school children in the sample has been collected from the teachers and schools concerned. The mothers rarely knew a great deal about the children's progress at school, the size of the class, amenities of the school, etc. Questions on the children's education told us more about the mother's relationship with the school and the teachers. Thus, the information in this study is based on eight-six interviews with mothers and another eighty with fathers or on behalf of fathers. It refers to their 617 children, for 398 of whom additional information was collected from schools.

Characteristics of the Families Interviewed

Twenty-nine, or over a third, of the families were newcomers to London in the sense that both parents had been born and had spent their childhood outside London. Less than a quarter of the families had lived in the same borough all their lives. The number of their children varied from five to fourteen. As many as eighteen of the eighty-six families had nine or more surviving children. But not all the children were dependent. As many as twenty of the families had teenage children who were working and who paid contributions to the mother while living at home. None of these children were in families with fathers whose occupations placed them in the Registrar General's social classes I and II. The distribution by social class of the sample compared with the distribution in London generally, shows rather more of the fathers in the large families belonged to social classes IV and V and rather fewer to social class II. These differences were not however statistically significant.

TABLE 1

Number and Percentage of Fathers in Families, According to Social Class

Occupational class of economically active males	Fathers in Survey 1965/6		All males Greater London Conurbation 1961
	N.	%	%
I Professional	5	6	5
II Managerial	7	8	16
III Skilled non-manual	4	} 48	52
III Skilled manual	37		
IV Semi-skilled manual	21	24	18
V Unskilled manual	12	14	9
Total	86[1]	100	100[2]

(1) This figure includes the two fatherless families where the mother's social class has been taken to be that of the absent father.
(2) Source: Census 1961. England and Wales Occupation Tables. General Register Office London. H.M.S.O. 1966, Table 27, p. 193.
These figures, based on a ten per cent sample, include all economically active males whether head of households or not, the sick and unemployed who are expecting to work again and the retired. It was not possible to exclude the retired to show a more useful comparison.

The variations in occupational status correspond with variations of income. Altogether, in sixty-six of the eighty-six families a father was in full-time employment. In table 2, we show the level of earnings of the father. In a quarter of these he earned less than £16 per week. But in nearly a third, he earned more than £25 per week. The table also shows the findings from the Ministry of Social Security survey. The two sets of figures are not directly comparable, because the Ministry's information was collected nationally in July 1966, whereas our information was collected in London in 1965-66 and includes relatively more families consisting of five children. But earnings of those with five and those with six or more children are very similar. The fact that more of the London fathers received earnings of more than £25 per week is partly because salary—and wage-levels are higher in London than elsewhere.[22]

Outline of the Study

The first part of the study describes the families' level of living. The families' general level of income and the different components

---

22. In 1965, 25 per cent of male employees in London earned over £25 per week, compared with 15 per cent in the United Kingdom as a whole. Ministry of Labour, *Family Expenditure Survey, Report for 1965,* London, H.M.S.O., p. 99.

of income are discussed in Chapter 2. In Chapter 3 we describe the families' housing and living conditions and show how in the private market poor housing is asssociated with low income but in local authority housing size of family is the overriding factor which determines the standard of the families' accommodation.

TABLE 2

Number and Percentage of Fathers in Full-time Work
by Range of Weekly Earnings

	Father in Full-time Employment			
Range of Weekly Earnings	Survey Families		Ministry of Social Security Survey*	
	N.	%	No. represented by sample	%
Under £16	20	27	43·100	27
£16 but less than £20	7	12	42·500	27
£20 „ „ „ £25	21	31	42·900	27
Over £25	18	30	30·800	19
Total	66	100	159·300	100
Median Earnings	£20 10s.		approx. £18 17s.	

* Fathers with five or more children only. Table A.4, *Circumstances of Families, op. cit.*

In the next two chapters the families' internal organization is described. There were many variations in the division of management and labour both between the parents and between parents and children. We discuss how money responsibilities were shared between the father and the mother in Chapter 4 and Chapter 5 how the household was run. The extent to which these responsibilities were interchangeable between various members of the family either regularly or in emergencies depended to some extent on the families' contacts with parents and siblings so the families' relationships with neighbours, workmates and school friends in the wider community are examined in Chapter 6. The families' dealings with officials from various authorities and welfare agencies are discussed in chapter 7.

The parent's own feelings about having a large family are described in Chapter 8. This includes a discussion about how the parents feel about their present situation and the extent to which the compensation of a large family makes up for material deprivation. The parents' attempts to limit their fertility and their reasons for their failure to do so are also explored in this chapter.

Finally Chapter 9 summarizes the main conclusions.

2. LEVELS AND SOURCES OF INCOMES

What was the standard of living of the families studied? This chapter attempts to answer this question by describing the amounts and sources of their income and by relating their total *regular* incomes to the cost of meeting a family's requirements as used by the National Assistance Board[1] at the time of the study. Two types of income deficiency were found—one long term and the other temporary though often recurrent.

The Extent of Income Deficiency

Sources of income were classified in the following categories:

(i) the father's basic wage or salary and family allowances, or, if he was not working, the state cash benefits paid to him and his family,

(ii) the father's overtime earnings,

(iii) the mother's earnings, and

(iv) the contributions to their parents of children living at home who were in paid employment.

The total of these items comprised regular weekly household income. Excluded from regular weekly income and discussed later in the chapter were welfare and education benefits in cash and kind, miscellaneous income in kind and iregular cash income. Each total was then expressed as a percentage of the basic National Assistance scale for that family. In line with the Ministry of Social Security's study, the family's actual housing costs were added to the total allowances for parents and dependent children.[2] It should be borne in mind that the sum calculated in this way is not necessarily what would have been granted if the family had actually claimed National Assistance. If the total allowances for a family had exceeded the Board's calculation of the father's 'normal' earnings, the family would

---

1. This was the measure used by the Ministry of Social Security in its study of families, to determine whether or not a family's financial resources were adequate. The rates in operation at the time of the study were 125s. 6d. for a married couple, with increases of 33s. 6d. for children aged 11 to 15, 27s. for chilisten 5 to 10, and 22s. 6d. for children under 5. (Housing costs are treated separately).

2. The National Assistance Board only paid interest payments on a mortgage, so for a few of the higher income families the level is over estimated.

be wage-stopped, i.e. their allowances reduced to bring the total to the 'normal' earnings of the father.[3] This study showed how difficult it is to define 'normal' earnings.

Eighteen families, nearly one in four of those interviewed, had a regular income below basic national assistance scales (see Table 2.1). Eleven of these families were mainly dependent on state benefits; in seven of them the father was in full time work. Another thirty-one (39 per cent) had incomes less than 40 per cent higher than the basic scale. At the other extreme were nine relatively prosperous large families with incomes more than double the scale.

TABLE 2.1

Number and Percentage of Families with Household Incomes Above and Below the National Assistance Basic Scale

Total regular household income as percentage of national assistance scale plus rent	Total number of dependent children				All families	
	5	6	7	8	N.	%
Under 80 per cent	1	–	2	1	4	5
80, less than 100	3	5	1	5	14	17
100, ,, ,, 120	3	3	7	2	15	19
120, ,, ,, 140	3	2	6	5	16	20
140, ,, ,, 160	2	4	2	–	8	10
160, ,, ,, 180	1	4	5	1	11	14
180, ,, ,, 200	1	1	–	1	3	4
over 200	4	3	2	–	9	11
Total	18	22	25	15	80	100

Note: Income data were not complete for six families.

The proportion with 'resources less than requirements' (22 per cent) was broadly confirmed by the survey carried out by the Ministry of Social Security. It is shown in Table 2.2 that in 1966, 20 per cent of families with five children and 26 per cent of families with six or more

TABLE 2.2

Percentage of Families of Different Size, with Resources Below Requirements by Occupational Status

Numbers of children	All types of family	Families with a father	
		in full-time work	sick or unemployed
2	5·1	1·3	46·2
3	7·2	2·2	62·0
4	11·1	3·9	84·6
5	19·7	7·4	87·3
6 or more	26·1	14·2	84·1
All families	7·4	2·4	63·1

Source: Tables III.3 and III.4, Ministry of Social Security, *Circumstances of Families, op. cit.*

---

3. The Board's calculation of 'normal' earnings was based on a man's probable *future* earnings rather than his *past* earnings. 'In calculating a man's probable future earnings, overtime, bonus pay and tips, if appropriate, are taken into account when it seems likely that they will form part of his regular future earnings. *This is something that is not always easy to decide.*' Personal communication from the National Assistance Board. (Author's italics.).

children in Britain had incomes, *before receipt of National Assistance,* which were below the basic assistance scales.[4]

The variations in absolute incomes among the eighty-six families is shown in Table 2.3. The family with the highest income received £7,000 per annum while the family with the lowest received less than £600. The median weekly income was £24 16s. This compares with a national mean income of £25 8s for households consisting of man and wife and three or more children, and, because London earnings are consistently higher than in the rest of the country, this suggests that earnings of men with large families, despite their higher average age, are relatively low.[5] The national mean income is only 10 per cent higher than the median weekly household income for all households in 1965.[6] The table shows that median income increases very little with additional children.

A substantial proportion of families had lower total incomes than average families with two children. The Family Expenditure Survey for 1965 shows that the median weekly household income (net of income tax and National Insurance contributions) of a married couple with two children was £22 6s.[7] Without knowing the 'cost' of a child at various ages in relation to the 'cost' of an adult it is impossible to state precisely how much worse off than the average family these large families are or how much more than £22 a family with at least five children needs to maintain a similar standard of living to the average two-child family. However, it is certainly true to say that the thirty-one large families (39 per cent) with regular

TABLE 2.3

Number and Percentage of Families by Range of Regular Weekly Household Income

Regular weekly household income	Number of dependent and non-dependent children					All families[1]	
	5	6	7	8	9+	N.	%
Under £15	4	2	–	–	1	7	9
£15 and less than £20	1	4	2	5	3	15	19
£20 ,, ,, ,, £22/3	1	2	3	2	1	9	11
£22/3 ,, ,, ,, £25	2	3	2	2	4	13	16
£25 ,, ,, ,, £30	3	1	2	4	5	15	19
£30 ,, ,, ,, £35	1	3	2	1	2	9	11
£35 and over	2	3	4	2	1	12	15
Total	14	18	15	16	17	80	100
Median Income	£22 16s.	£23 13s.	£25 4s.	£24 12s.	£24 12s.	£24 2s.	

(1) All families exclude six for whom income was unknown.

4. It should be noted that the Ministry did not give statistics (a) showing the distribution of incomes, other than tables showing how many families were within £1, £2 or £3 of the basic national assistance scale, and (b) showing levels of resources *after* receipt of assistance. Since large families, even if they receive national assistance, tend to receive payments reduced because of the 'wage-stop' the figures in the second column of Table 2.2 for families with four or more children are likely to be only a little smaller when National Assistance is taken into account.
5. Ministry of Labour *Family Expenditure Survey, Report for 1965,* London, H.M.S.O., Table 13, p. 88.
6. *Ibid.,* Table 2, p. 29.
7. *Ibid.,* Table 12, p. 83.

weekly money incomes of less than £22 3s were worse off than the average two-child family. Seven families with incomes less than £15 4s or the lower quartile for the two-child family were very much worse off.

Supplements to Income

How far did the poorest families have supplementary sources of income? In addition to current cash income (of the four kinds listed above) the following were also ascertained:

(v) welfare and education benefits in cash and kind;
(vi) irregular money income such as casual earnings, financial windfalls of an unpredictable nature, for example winnings on football pools, or a legacy, and money drawn from savings; and
(vii) miscellaneous income in kind, such as gifts of clothing from family and friends, schoolchildren's earnings and gifts from employers.

(Welfare benefits have been given a weekly cash value when possible[8] and where money was received on an irregular basis, the amount has been averaged over a year to give a weekly amount.)

TABLE 2.4

Percentage of Families with Income above and below National Assistance Scales, according to Cumulative Definitions of Income

Percentage of N.A.B. scale rates plus rent	Basic wage or state benefits and family allowances I	I plus overtime earnings II	II plus wife's earnings III	III plus children's contributions IV	IV plus welfare and education in kind V	V plus irregular money income VI	VI plus income in kind VII
Under 80	29	9	6	5	–	–	–
80– 89	29	16	12	8	6	6	4
90– 99	13	11	11	10	12	10	12
100–109	5	9	8	9	12	14	14
110–119	5	6	12	10	10	8	3
120–129	3	13	12	14	12	11	15
130–139	2	4	2	6	6	10	11
140–159	3	15	12	10	11	10	9
160–199	2	6	14	17	18	16	17
200+	9	11	11	11	11	15	15
Total	100	100	100	100	100	100	100
Number	71*	80	80	80	80	80	80

Note: Regular current household income – IV
Horizontal line – median

* Excludes nine families not dependent on a basic wage, but only on self employed or piece-rate earnings. They have been included in II – VII.

8. See p. 25 for a fuller explanation.

19

However, the addition of income in kind and irregular money income only raised five of the eighteen families from points below the National Assistance scales to points above them. Table 2.4 shows in some detail the cumulative effect upon living standards of taking account of the different sources of income.

Thirty one of the families would have had an insufficient income but for overtime earnings and the earnings of the mother. In sixty-six of eighty-six families the father was in paid employment. Table 2.5 shows the proportion of families with other sources of income to supplement the father's basic wage and shows the largest source of such income. The sample is small but it would seem that when the basic wage or salary is relatively high (in the case of this survey over £20 per week) there are less likely to be overtime earnings or mother's earnings. Perhaps the pressures on men to work overtime and on mothers to supplement the wage are less. The results of the Ministry of Social Security's survey suggest also, that the pressures on fathers of large families to work long hours, and on mothers to supplement his earnings are greater than for parents of small families.[9]

TABLE 2.5

Number of Families with Fathers Receiving Different Basic Wages, who had a Secondary Source of Income

Largest source of income additional to father's basic wage or salary	Basic wage or salary of father				All families with father as wage earner	
	£10/£13	£14/£15	£16/£19	£20+	N.	%
None	3	1	1	7	12	21
Overtime	9	12	7	1	29	51
Mother's earnings	5	3	2	–	10	17
Children's contribution	3	1	–	–	4	7
Pension	1	–	–	1	2	4
Total	21	17	10	9	57	100

Note: Nine families not dependent on a basic wage or salary but only upon self-employed or piece-rate earnings have been excluded.

Fluctuating Income Levels

How far were families in long-term as distinct from temporary poverty? This depended largely on the health of the father. The circumstances of fourteen of the eighteen families with incomes

---

9. The Ministry of Social Security study found that 23 per cent of men in full-time work with five children and 21 per cent with six or more compared with 14 per cent of men with two children, worked 60 or more hours weekly. *Circumstances of Families, op. cit.*, p. 40. The proportion of working mothers was found to decrease from one in three amongst two-child families to one in four amongst families with six children, and the average amount earned was lower among the latter. Nevertheless 1 per cent of families with two children would have had incomes below national assistance basic level if the mother had stopped working compared with 7 per cent of families with five children and 4 per cent with six or more children. *Ibid.* p. 33. It is also interesting to note that among families where there were children under school age, the proportion of mothers in employment was less (21 per cent compared with 32 per cent of all families); but in very large families the proportion were nearly the same (21 per cent and 23 per cent respectively) *Ibid.* p. 34.

below the National Assistance scales had not changed significantly during the previous year. Seven of them were families with a father in full time work. These were men who either lacked the skills to command a job with high basic wages or the health or opportunity to work long hours to supplement low basic wages. Their situation was unlikely to change for the better. Another seven had been unemployed or sick. There was little prospect of their situation changing in the near future because they suffered from ill health which had severely reduced their working capacities. However, the circumstances of four had changed in the last few months and they were likely to move out of income poverty once the father was able to return to full-time employment. For example, one man had had an accident and broken his arm, another was at home looking after his wife while she had another baby. The drop in his family's income was also temporary.

Account must also be taken of the families with incomes higher than the National Assistance scales. For example, nine families had experienced poverty in recent months because the father had had periods off work due to illness. Furthermore, the illnesses of eight of these fathers was of a recurrent nature: particularly because of chest and heart trouble. Not only were they likely to experience repeated periods off work[10] but also periods when their working capacity was reduced. In these families overtime was therefore an unreliable source of income. A further two fathers had experienced redundancy followed by a period of unemployment and a third father had spent six weeks looking after the children during the mother's illness. Other families lived precariously in the sense that their living standard depended upon contributions from a mother's earning or from irregular sources which might easily terminate. In effect, some families were just above National Assistance level because of some 'unreliable' source of income. This was an important finding of the research and needs to be discussed in relation to different sources of income.

Basic Wages

Sixty-six, or 82 per cent, of the families as already noted had a father who was in full time work. The proportion is itself significant, as it is lower than found for families of smaller size.[11] The greater vulnerability to sickness and unemployment of the father of large

---

10. The Ministry of Social Security study found that 35 per cent of fathers in full-time work with two children had been absent from work at least once in the twelve months preceding the survey, compared with 50 per cent of fathers with six or more children. These results indicate that a large family's income is more precarious than that of a smaller family. *Circumstances of Families, op. cit.*, p. 43.
11. In their national survey the Ministry of Social Security found that 85 per cent of fathers with five or more children, and 83 per cent of fathers with six or more children, compared with 94 per cent of fathers with two children, were in full-time employment. 'The proportion of fathers of five or more children who were off work was more than twice the proportion among the fathers of smaller families.' *Ibid.*, pp. 19–21 (Percentages calculated from data about standard families in Table III.3.).

families may be due, in part, to their being older than fathers of small families.[12]

Seven of the sixty-six families had an income below the National Assistance scale; and if none of the families interviewed had been able to supplement their basic wages or salary the number below the scale would have been thirty-eight (excluding the self-employed or piece-rate worker, as it was not possible to calculate a 'basic wage'). The unskilled workers had precarious incomes as several were outdoor workers and their earnings fell during bad weather. Table 2.6 shows how far below the basic scale some families would have fallen. In fact, the median value of basic wages for all the families in this study was 12 per cent less than the basic National Assistance scales.

TABLE 2.6

Basic Wages of Fathers in Full-time Employment by Range in Relation to the Basic National Assistance Level

Basic Wage (net of NI Contribution) and Family Allowance as percentage of national assistance scale	Number of Fathers in Full-time employment
Under 60	1
60– 69	5
70– 79	13
80– 89	12
90– 99	7
100–109	5
110–119	4
120–139	1
140–199	3
200 and over	6
Total	57
Median Percentage	88

Note: Nine families who were self-employed or paid on piece-rates earnings are excluded.

In the previous year fourteen fathers had been off work for periods varying from a week to six months—twelve for reasons of ill-health and two because of redundancy. They were all in work when interviewed and twelve of them had basic wage rates below basic National Assistance scales. These families could not be certain of maintaining their income above the basic scales, especially as eight fathers suffered from heart-trouble or bronchitis—illnesses likely to reduce working capacity, as well as making it less possible for them to take on extra work.

---

12. The numbers in this sample are too small to test this. The Ministry of Social Security did not include information on the ages of the fathers in their analysis. The fathers of the large families who suffered from chronic or recurrent ill health were on average 44 years old; two years older than the sample as a whole. However this difference was not statistically significant.

Overtime earnings

Overtime earnings raised the median income from 88 per cent to 116 per cent of the basic National Assistance level and were extremely important for a large proportion of families. In fact, they formed the largest secondary source of income for twenty-nine, or over one-third, of all the families in the sample. Only one father had a regular second job. Nearly a third (twenty-one) of the working fathers worked over fifty hours a week, nine of them over sixty hours. Overtime accounted for between a quarter and a half of the total household income for ten of the families and over half for two of them. The poorest families were those in which the father was unable, through ill-health or the nature of his job, to work overtime. For example, Mr. Radley[13] was a gardener and worked for the local council. In the summer he could sometimes earn a little extra by doing private gardening but in the winter this was impossible. Mr. Burton, on the other hand, was a builder's labourer who rarely managed to work more than a total of forty hours a week as he was epileptic and so lost a lot of time. He remained in work by keeping his affliction a secret from his employer. If he had a fit during the day he had to hide.

Even if the father usually worked overtime there were times when he had to rely solely on his basic wage. For example, although he might have been entitled to holiday pay this was usually at his basic wage rate. This made a holiday away doubly difficult for the large family and instead some fathers found an extra job to help them over the holiday period. At the birth of a new baby, the father was the most likely person to stay at home to look after the children: the father had looked after the children at the birth of the last baby in two-thirds of the families. The majority (forty-eight) of the fathers were able to arrange to take their holiday over this period and so received holiday pay. Five had found they were not entitled to holiday pay, and so had applied for National Assistance. They had found this was not always easily obtained.[14]

Mothers' and Children's earnings

The mother's earnings allowed some families to escape poverty, and for ten of the eighty families such earnings were the largest source of 'secondary' income (Table 2.5). Nineteen of the mothers (nearly one in four) had jobs, eight of them full-time.[15] The most usual part-time job (twenty hours weekly on average) was cleaning.

---

13. The real names of the families interviewed in this study have not been used, fictitious names have been used throughout the report.
14. Their difficulties are discussed in greater detail in Chapter 7, p. 112.
15. The families in this small sample were typical of large families in Britain in this respect. In their survey throughout Britain the Ministry of Social Security found 25 per cent of mothers in families with six children where the father was in full-time employment, were in work. *Circumstances of Families, op. cit.*, p. 33.

This meant either starting work at four or five in the morning and returning home in time to get breakfast for the family, or working in the evenings, leaving the father or elder children to look after the family. One remarkable mother looked after her five children (aged between 3 and 11) during the day, and worked all night. She had been doing this for ten years: 'You feel like an automaton, everything is so finely timed you just go from one thing to the next without thinking about it. I'd miss it if I stopped though.'

Mother's earnings were unreliable as a source of income, because work could be interrupted not only by childbirth but whenever any member of the family was sick or had an accident. Furthermore, the more children a woman has had the greater the chance of complications occurring at the birth of the next baby. For example, one mother had been ill for six weeks at the birth of her last baby. Some of the families therefore whose total income was only just above the National Assistance level at the time of the survey were liable to fall below this level recurrently. One mother had high blood pressure and there were times when she could not work, nevertheless she refused to give up the cleaning job because the family badly needed the money. Moreover, families with higher incomes were still vulnerable. In seven families the mother's earnings accounted for more than a quarter of the household income; three families would have fallen below the basic scale if the mother had stopped working. Some mothers, earning only £4 or £5 cleaning, raised the family's income above the level at which they would have qualified for free school meals, uniform grants, rent and rate rebates and other benefits. After taking into account the extra expense involved in getting to work, meals out and the strain involved, it is debatable whether the family would have been better off if she had not taken employment.

It seemed that once one or more of the children began working mothers tended to give up their own jobs. In only two of the twenty-two families having an older child who was at work did the mother work as well. Generally speaking, however, the value of the child's contribution to the households was small: rarely more than £3 per week. This covered the cost of their food but little more.

State cash benefits

As many as fourteen, or one in six families, were dependent on state benefits—a much higher proportion than would be expected among small families. First there were seven families in which the father was out of work and unlikely to work again at his former occupation owing to chronic illness. Six were receiving an income below and only one of them an income above the basic National Assistance scale. The father of this family received an Army pension in addition to National Assistance. The chronic sick included an epileptic, two suffering from severe heart trouble, three from bronchitis and one from tuberculosis. If they were considered capable of work, it was only as light labourers and so their assumed normal earnings were based on the wages of a light labourer, which in 1965 were very low.[16]

Second were five families in which the father was temporarily off work either because of his own or the mother's ill health. Three of them received less than *80 per cent* and one less than 100 per cent of the basic National Assistance scale. The only family in this category to keep above the basic National Assistance scale did so because the mother took on a second cleaning job rather than go to the National Assistance Board to seek supplementation of sickness benefit. One man had been at home for three months because his wife had broken her leg three months before their ninth baby was born and had been told by her doctors to rest and stay off her feet as much as possible. He and a mate had a lorry and sold scrap iron; in the summer business was good and he could bring home £30 a week but in the winter he sometimes only made £8 or £9. He had the impression it was better to under-estimate his earnings, so the National Assistance Board had taken his 'normal' earnings to be about £11. Thus his total weekly income (including family allowances) throughout the winter on which to keep a wife and six children (he had two children in care) had been £13 5s or £5 below the basic National Assistance scales.

Third were two fatherless families. One was only temporarily fatherless while the father was visiting Pakistan. The other was a family in which the mother was legally separated from the father. The incomes of these two families were much closer to basic scales, because a fatherless family is not subject to the wage-stop.

The Equivalent cash value of Education and Welfare benefits

The value of benefits to which families in need are entitled is considerable, and (apart from free or subsidised holidays) it is possible to give them a cash value. The potential value of these benefits may be four or five times that of family allowances. For example, a child who stays on at school over the leaving age can receive *free*

---

16 The Supplementary Benefits Commission's survey of fifty-two wage-stopped families in Autumn 1967 found only a third were in good health and nineteen were actually registered disabled. One in three had had their benefit reduced by more than £2 10s. See *Administration of the Wage Stop*, London, H.M.S.O., December 1967. Since April 1968 the earning capacity of labourers and light labourers has been assessed on the basis of local authority wage rates and the 7s 6d deduction for expenses incurred because of being in employment, removed. This initially benefitted 14,000 claimants: about half the total number of wage-stop families. Local authority wage-rates are low. A survey by the National Board of Prices and Incomes in October 1966 found that full-time manual workers of local authorities earned a minimum of £11 11s. A quarter of them were earning less than £13 1s. and the median income was £15 2s. For this and the distribution of earnings of other occupations see Department of Employment and Productivity. *A National Minimum Wage, An Inquiry*, London, H.M.S.O., 1969. Appendix VI, p. 77.

school meals, an *education maintenance· allowance* and *uniform grant* which could be worth a total of forty shillings a week.

The value of a free school meal has been taken to be one shilling. This does not include the overall subsidy on each meal which is valued at approximately 1s 6d per meal.[17] Every child who receives a school dinner is subsidised to this extent, but this general subsidy has not been added to the families' incomes in Table 2.4. The welfare milk tokens to which all pregnant mothers and children under the age of five are entitled (each token worth 4d a day) and the cash value of the one-third of a pint of milk per day each schoolchild is entitled to receive has been treated in the same way. Only the cash value of *extra* milk tokens to which low income families are entitled have been included in Table 2.4.[18] Only the specific education and welfare benefits which are given to make up for a family's inadequate income have been included for the purpose of comparing the large families' income in this study.[19]

A cash value has not been placed on free or subsidised holidays because an estimate is difficult to make. A free holiday did not save the family any money as the child would not have had a holiday at all if it had not been free. The value of the meals the child had whilst away could be estimated but the sum involved would not be very large. Besides, when a child went on holiday the family was involved in extra expenses it would not otherwise have had: extra pocket money, a swimming costume, say, or some new clothing, which makes the element of 'real' subsidy extremely difficult to calculate. The non-monetary value of a holiday in any case could be argued to outweigh any cash value. The more restricted the child's home environment the more 'valuable' a holiday away becomes. It is interesting to note, however, that subsidised holidays were not restricted to the lower income groups.[20]

Irregular money incomes

Only six families had obtained casual earnings in the previous year. The work varied from painting and decorating during holiday periods, looking after a neighbour's children while the usual child-minder was ill, to 'going on the fiddle'—i.e. buying and selling jewellery illegally in Petticoat Lane. The amount of money earned in this way was sometimes sufficient to finance a family holiday.

Altogether, twenty-seven families had received a *financial windfall*

---

17. Since this survey was completed the price of school meals has increased to 1s. 6d, and the overall subsidy on each meal is valued at approximately 1s. 4d.
18. The importance of welfare and school milk to the children's diet is discussed in Chapter 4.
19. The main purpose of this study was not to compare the value of subsidies in cash or kind received by large families as compared with small families and households with no children. Many other benefits ranging from the value of tax allowances, the Health Services and the Education Services would have to be assessed and taken into account. This would be a complicated and difficult task and would be a major study in itself.
20. Holidays are further discussed in Chapter 7, pp. 103–104.

of some kind in the past twelve months. For some this was a legacy, for others money presents from the family and for still others winnings on the horses or football pools. One woman said she never worried about meeting extra bills because she always came up on the horses when extra money had to be found. A lucky win had bought the eldest boy's school uniform. Betting could be one of the only ways of financing purchases of clothing and household goods. If it was unsuccessful the family went without. The two richest families in the study had also had the largest financial windfalls.

Four families had drawn money from their savings. Sometimes this was to meet an emergency. One professional man who had resigned from his job on a matter of principle had been unemployed for six weeks. During this time he spent £200 from his savings to supplement unemployment benefit. On the other hand, one wife had been drawing on her savings nearly every week because she regularly spent £2 or £3 more than the weekly housekeeping money her husband gave her. Together with the money they had spent repairing and decorating the house to which they had moved they had spent £300 of their savings in two years.

The average value of irregular money ranged from 8s to £20 a week; again the family with the highest regular money income also had the largest irregular income.

Miscellaneous income in kind

This was the most difficult form of income to measure in cash terms. However, for some families it was considerable, and as with education and welfare benefits, it was not the families with the lowest money income who received the most in kind.

Seventeen families reported substantial and frequent *gifts of clothing* from family, friends or a voluntary agency. Children's clothing was passed around between families in most income groups, but the information collected suggested that it was only in the poorer families that the mother wore many secondhand clothes. Many of the poorer mothers had to buy their clothing at jumble sales, for only four of the eighteen families with a regular money income below the basic National Assistance scale were frequently given clothing. Seven of the thirty-two families with regular money income above 140 per cent of the basic National Assistance scale had substantial gifts of clothing: the same proportion as among the poorest families.

Among the 420 schoolchildren in the eighty families 160 were secondary schoolchildren. Thirty of these earned small weekly sums by doing paper rounds, helping the milkman or working in a shop on Saturdays. The amount earned varied between 16s and 30s. The cash was not handed over to their mothers. Sometimes it was saved to buy a new pair of shoes, a pair of jeans or, like their older working brothers and sisters, it was used to buy treats for the young children as well as for themselves. Pocket money earned in this way undoubtedly increased the family's level of living because parents' expenditure on both younger and older children could be increased. The amount earned by the children has been included as income in kind when considering the level of the *family* income.

A few children were given pocket money by relatives, friends or, in one case a teacher. These amounts, rarely worth more than 5s a week, have also been included as income in kind.

A few fathers were able to bring home goods received in connection with their work. For example, a furniture porter was sometimes given curtains, blankets, clothes by customers who no longer needed them; a shoe mender was given free tickets to the local cinema because his employer advertised this cinema in his shop. Lorry or van drivers were occasionally allowed to have petrol. However, although such benefits were received by families in all income groups, the more substantial fringe benefits (meal vouchers or subsidised meals, free travel) were more likely to be found in the higher income groups. Only one family had a flat provided rent free by the man's employers.

Summary

The families in this study can be divided into three broad groups on the basis of the level and source of their income. The first group consists of eighteen (or 22 per cent) of the families with regular money incomes below the level of the National Assistance basic scales. These families depended either on low basic wages or state benefits, supplemented only by family allowances. The addition of income in kind and irregular money income only raised five of them above the basic National Assistance scales, leaving thirteen families with a total income in cash and kind below these scales. The families receiving considerable help in cash or in kind from relatives or friends and occasionally supplementary income from various sources were usually the relatively better off families.

The second group were the thirty-one families, representing another 39 per cent of the sample, who had incomes above the basic scales at the time of the interview but whose standard of living was precarious. If the father were to lose the opportunity or ability to do overtime or the mother were to give up her paid employment, the family's income would fall to the level of the father's basic wage which even with family allowances would be below the National Assistance basic scales. Twelve of these families had had just this experience in the previous year. Eight, one in four, of the fathers in this group also had illnesses of a recurrent nature such as bronchitis or heart trouble, and all of them had experienced periods off work off in the past twelve months. In effect, these families were potential members of the first group.

The remaining group of thirty-one families (39 per cent) had sufficiently high basic wages or salaries to keep the family income safely above the National Assistance basic scales. Even in times of sickness or unemployment they could expect to maintain their level of living for some time because their employers had generous sick pay schemes or they had resources of their own. These families could be regarded as having adequate stable incomes. But they were a minority of the total sample.

We find then that the crucial elements in a family's level of living are the father's basic wage or salary and family allowances. The median value of these was only 88 per cent of the National Assistance basic scales. Overtime earnings raised the median to 116 per cent, but this in itself shows the importance of the ability of the father of a large family to work overtime. For the worker who lacks skill or suffers from poor health not only are basic wages low but his ability to do overtime is limited. In 9 per cent of the families the father was chronically sick or disabled and in another 7 per cent he was sick or unemployed at the time of the interview. In more than another 20 per cent he had experienced sickness or unemployment in the past year and income had in most families been reduced sharply for short periods.

Two types of financial deprivation were therefore found among the large families in this study: one long term and the other temporary though often recurrent. *Thirty* families (35 per cent) had experienced one or other type in the past year, including 16 per cent who were perpetually below National Assistance basic scales.[21] In the majority of instances an underlying factor was the ill health or disability of the father, for it helped to account for dependence on low basic wage or state benefits.

---

21. This includes 12 fathers with basic wage below the basic scale who, although working at the time of the survey, had been off work in the previous year, four fathers who were temporarily off work at the time of the survey, and fourteen who were permanently poor. (See previous sections on basic wages and state cash benefits).

A family's living standards depend partly on the quality of its environment. Housing is one aspect of this environment which can to some extent be measured. Three aspects of housing can be measured objectively: the living space available to the family; the amenities in the house; and some facts about its surroundings which are particularly important to a family with several young children. How did the accommodation of the large families in this study compare with other families when examined in these ways? Were the problems facing them just those of overcrowding? Had their accommodation problems worsened as the family had grown in size or had they experienced more severe problems of a different kind in the past?

TABLE 3.1

Number and Percentage of Families who are Tenants and Owner Occupiers

Tenure	Household Income as per cent of National Assistance Scale			All families[1]	
	under 100	100 but less than 140	140 and over	N	%
Council tenant	16	23	13	56	65
Private tenant	2	4	4	10	12
Owner occupier	—	4	14	20	23
Total	18	31	31	86	100

(1) All families include six for whom income was unknown.

The proportion of owner-occupiers (23 per cent) was lower than would have been found among smaller families.[1] Not all of these families who were owner-occupiers had chosen this form of tenure. Two families had inherited the house in which they were living and both were hoping to move into larger accommodation. Four owner-occupiers had taken on a financial commitment which they could only meet either by letting part of their accommodation or by

---

1. The proportion of owner-occupiers was significantly lower than other householders at the 1 per cent level. In the Greater London conurbation in 1964, 38 per cent of households were owner-occupiers. Ministry of Labour *Family Expenditure Survey, Report for 1964.* London, H.M.S.O., 1965, p.7.

supplementing their income by the father working overtime or the mother going out to work. Dependence on an unreliable source of income could lead a family into considerable difficulty, as one family had discovered.

The Blooms had fallen into financial difficulties because Mr. Bloom had become redundant during the previous year and had spent two weeks on unemployment benefit and National Assistance before taking a job at which he earned much less because there was no chance to work overtime. The National Assistance Board only paid the interest element of their mortgage payments so they had fallen behind and had not been able to catch up afterwards because of the large drop in earnings. They had not set out to buy the house. They had first moved in when it had been requisitioned by the council. When it had become de-requisitioned the original owner at first had wanted to increase the rent or evict the Blooms. He then offered to sell it to them as sitting tenants, to which the Blooms had agreed because they felt it was the only way to be sure of a roof over their heads. As Mr. Bloom said, 'They panicked us into buying it—they were using us a prawns (sic) in the game. I wouldn't recommend a family like us to do it—to buy a house.' They managed while Mr. Bloom had a secure job but the previous year's difficulties had thrown them into confusion. At the time of the survey Mrs. Bloom had taken on night work to help catch up on some of their debts.

Three other families were West Indians who had each resorted to buying their home because of the difficulty of finding rented accommodation. Each family was sharing the house with another tenant. One family had no choice because the only house they could afford contained a sitting tenant and the other two needed the money to help pay their high housing costs. Even so the housing costs of one of these families represented half of the household income, which included the mother's earnings.

Tenants of private landlords were a minority. Among the ten families renting accommodation not belonging to a local authority, two were sharing their parents' accommodation and three lived in accommodation owned by their employers. One of the latter was living rent free. None of the families were living in furnished rented accommodation at the time of the survey. Only one was a rent controlled tenant. Eight of the families were on a council housing list. The large families had clearly been given priority in obtaining council accommodation as nearly two-thirds were council tenants.[2]

2. The large families in this study were similar in this respect to the large families in the Ministry of Social Security's study of families throughout Great Britain. In families with the father in full-time work 52 per cent of those with five children and 60 per cent of those with six or more children were council tenants. Only 26 per cent of families with two children lived in local authority property. Ministry of Social Security *op cit.* p. 54, Table VI.3. Where the father was sick or unemployed the proportions were higher. 74 per cent of familes with four or more children and 50 per cent of families with two or three children were council tenants. Ministry of Social Security *Circumstances of Families*, *op. cit.*, p. 55, Table VI.4.

But when their housing history is examined it is clear that this 'priority' had been hard-earned.

The Families' Past Housing Experiences

'The people who suffered most from housing stress are those with the lowest incomes, those with average incomes and large families and many of the newcomers to London.'[3] As well as being large a third (twenty-nine) of the families in this study were newcomers to London (meaning both parents had been born and brought up outside London), and altogether thirty-one had incomes below average. Less than a quarter (eighteen) of the mothers said that they had never experienced any bad housing problems since their marriage, the majority (ten) of whom were owner-occupiers with weekly incomes above £25. The majority (fifty-eight) of the mothers said they had experienced their worst accommodation problems before the time of the survey usually when they had formally occupied privately rented furnished accommodation.

Half (fifteen) the newcomers in London and a third (twenty) of the Londoners in the study had experienced their worst problems when they were private tenants. Only a few (seven) families had had their worst difficulties at an earlier stage in their marriage, when they had been living with relatives.

Altogether a third (nineteen) of the council tenants had had very severe housing problems before they had been rehoused by a local authority, involving homelessness, family break up and breakdown in health. Moreover, they had not been helped until long after their situation had become critical. Ten families had been 'homeless' for periods ranging from six weeks to two years. The experience of Part III accommodation was one that none of the families had forgotten, '——————— ———, that was a terrible place—it drove me up the wall. The food was disgusting, it couldn't have been worse in a concentration camp. As for not letting your husband be with you— that was one of the worst parts. It's times like that when you're really up against it that you need to stick together,' said one mother. Another said that her eight year old daughter had started having nightmares while they were living there. Two years later (at the time of the survey), the girl would still sometimes wake up in the night screaming. Five families had had children in care[4] or living with relatives because they could not find accommodation for the

---

3. *Housing in Greater London* (The Milner Holland Report). The Report of the Committee on Housing in Greater London. London, H.M.S.O., Cmd. 2605, 1965, p. 81.
4. Between March 1965 and March 1966 in England and Wales no fewer than 3,610 children were received into the care of local authorities' children's committees because their families were homeless either through eviction or for other reasons. Home Office *Children in Care in England and Wales, March 1965–March 1966* Cmnd. 3204. London, H.M.S.O., 1967, Table 1.

whole family, and four mothers had suffered a breakdown in health which they attributed mainly to bad housing.

Altogether, thirteen families said they had been given council accommodation for health reasons. A further thirteen families had been moved out of property, due for demolition under slum clearance plans and fourteen families had previously been living in very over-crowded conditions.[5] The average length of time these families had waited on the housing list was seven years.

The Families' Present Housing Amenities

Mrs. Stanley and her eight children who lived on the first and second floor of a large house in North London were experiencing extreme conditions. The house looked less cared for than the other houses in the street; windows were broken and the paint was peeling. One of the broken windows had been half-heartedly boarded up with an old door. Mrs. Stanley told us that the cellars flooded easily and usually had three feet of water in them. In the summer the smell of this water was bad and during the previous winter rats had been found in the cellars. Mrs. Stanley had access to seven rooms but could not use two of them owing to damp. The flat had no running hot water, every drop of hot water needed for the family had to be heated in a kettle. There was a bath but the geyser was so old that the man who came to repair it laughed when he saw it and told her that the manufacturer had stopped making parts for that model many years ago. The fire in the kitchen smoked badly when the wind was in a certain direction which, as the Inspector of Health had noted was 'detrimental to health'. Mrs. Stanley had lived in this flat for nine years and had been trying to persuade the Council, which owned the property, to move her to better accommodation for some time.[6]

We used the twelve-point standard[7] which is based on recommenda-tions of the 1946 Standards of Fitness for Habitation Sub-Committee to measure the quality of the accommodation of the families. Altogether nearly half (forty) of the families were living in dwellings which were deficient in at least one respect. These families included all except two of the private tenants, nearly half (twenty-six) the council tenants but only one sixth of the owner-occupiers. Among them were eleven of these families (13 per cent of the total) who were living in accommodation which was below the standard of

---

5. 'Very overcrowded conditions' was not precisely defined but meant a family with five or six children living in two rooms, for example.
6. Mrs. Stanley has been rehoused since the survey took place. The public health inspector cannot take his own authorities to court as he could a private landlord. Rosalind Brooke uses this as an example of the more favoured position of local authorities in the legal system. See Rosalind Brooke, Civic Rights and Social Services. *The Political Quarterly*, Vol. 5140. No. 1, January 1969, p. 94.
7. This scale was used for administering the system of discretionary improvement grants payable under the Housing (Financial Provision) Act 1958. See Appendix 2.

minimum fitness.[8] These houses had been condemned and were due for demolition. Eight of them belonged to the council.

TABLE 3.2

Number and Percentage of Families with Different Incomes
Living in Substandard Accommodation

Standard of Dwelling	Household income as per cent of National Assistance Scale		All families[1]	
	Under 140	140 and over	N	%
Council tenants				
1. Substandard dwellings	17	8	25	31
2. Below minimum fitness	4	4	8	10
3. Not substandard	18	1	19	23
Private tenants				
1. Substandard dwellings	5	2	7	8
2. Below minimum fitness	1	2	3	4
3. Not substandard	–	–	–	–
Owner-Occupier				
1. Substandard dwellings	2	3	5	6
2. Below minimum fitness	–	–	–	–
3. Not substandard	2	11	13	16

(1) All families excludes six families for whom income was unknown.

The owner-occupiers had on the whole the best living conditions and the private tenants the worst (see Table 3.2). The high income council tenants were just as likely to have substandard accommodation as those with lower incomes. In the private market the poorer families were more likely to be living in substandard dwellings.

Nearly half (296) of the children in the survey were being brought up in homes lacking at least one amenity. The three amenities considered essential by the Dennington Committee were a fixed bath, a system for supplying hot water and a ventilated food cupboard. Altogether fifteen dwellings had no means of heating water except in a kettle on a stove, sixteen dwellings had no fixed bath and nineteen dwellings had no ventilated food cupboard or its equivalent. All the families said they missed hot water and their own bath; it can however be questioned whether a dwelling should be judged substandard because of the absence of adequate food storage facilities. Not only do many families not want one[9] but the poorer familiees lack the means to accumulate stocks of food and so do not need one. The mothers only bought enough food for each day and kept what little they had in a sideboard or kitchen cabinet. For

---

8. The Ministry of Social Security found in their study of families throughout Great Britain that 18 per cent of all families were living in defective dwellings· Among families with six or more children the proportion was 33 per cent. *Circumstances of Families, op. cit.,* p. 56, Table VI, 7.
9. 'Indeed I would go further and say that the evidence suggested that many families do not wish to have a ventilated food store and that when it is provided the ventilation is blocked up to keep out the dirt and the cold air.' Reservation by J. B. Cullingworth and D. V. Donnison, *Our Older Homes – A Call for Action,* report of Central Housing Advisory Committee, London, H.M.S.O., 1966, p. 39.

example, seven sliced loaves and some tins of tomato soup formed the bulk of one family's food supply, all of which was easily contained inside a kitchen cabinet. As one mother said: 'We live from day to day—what's the point of me having a fridge. I'd never have anything to put in it.'

Overcrowding

Most of the families were unable to obtain accommodation of sufficient size to meet their needs. In London large flats and houses are expensive in the private market and in short supply amongst council dwellings. Only the large families whose incomes were well above the average had obtained adequate accommodation.

We have used two measures of overcrowding in this study. The first, taken from the census defines an overcrowded dwelling as one in which there are more than one and a half persons per room. A kitchen is counted as a room if it is large enough to eat in. The second known as the 'bedroom standard' takes account of the age and sex of persons. It is assumed that two children under the age of ten can share a bedroom but those aged ten and under twenty-one must only share if the other is of the same sex. Each married couple and person aged twenty-one and over is assumed to require a room.[10] According to the census definition three quarters of the council tenants, all but two of the private tenants and a quarter of the owner-occupiers were overcrowded.

According to the bedroom standard 63 per cent of the families were overcrowded—nearly a fifth (sixteen) being short of two or more bedrooms and 44 per cent being short of one bedroom. These figures compare unfavourably with figures for all families. Only 25 per cent of families with children in primary schools were over-crowded by the bedroom standard.[11]

Families who owned their own houses (two-thirds of whom had a regular weekly income of over £30) were the most adequately housed. According to the census definition[12] only five were overcrowded and these were the families who had either been driven to take on the responsibilities of home ownership or had been left their house by a relative. At the other end of the private market all but one of the ten families living as private tenants were overcrowded. None of them, it must be pointed out had a weekly income of over £30.

The adequacy of the council tenants accommodation was not

10. For a further explanation see Appendix 2.
11. Amongst the families of social class V the proportion was nearer than for large families (43 per cent). *Children and their Primary Schools* (The Plowden Report). A report of the Central Advisory Council for Education (England) Vol. 2. Appendix 3. London, H.M.S.O., 1967, p. 124, Table 34. The difference between the proportion of overcrowded large families and all families with children was significant at the 0·001 level. The numbers of large families in each social class were too small to establish statistically significant differences between social classes.
12. The Census definition of overcrowding is only slightly less generous than the modified bedroom standard for the family with several children because the Census definition takes no account of age.

related to their income. The families with the lowest incomes were not more overcrowded than families with higher incomes. Whether a family in council accommodation was overcrowded or not depended principally on when they had moved into their present accommodation and whether they had had further children since the move.

TABLE 3.3

Number of Families with Different Incomes who lived in Overcrowded Accommodation

Tenure	Household income as per cent of National Assistance scale		All families[1]
	Under 140	140 and over	N
Council tenancy			52
1. More than $1\frac{1}{2}$ persons/room	29	10	39
2. Less than Bedroom standard	18	5	23
3. Overcrowded on neither criteria	10	3	13
Private tenancy			10
1. More than $1\frac{1}{2}$ persons/room	5	4	9
2. Less than Bedroom standard	2	1	3
3. Overcrowded on neither criteria	1	–	1
Owner-Occupier			18
1.More than $1\frac{1}{2}$ persons/room	3	3	6
2. Less than Bedroom standard	2	3	5
3. Overcrowded on neither criteria	1	11	12

(1) All families excludes six for whom income was unknown.

Only one family was overcrowded when they first moved into their present dwelling but fifty-one of the fifty-six families in Council accommodation had had further children since the move. The largest families (those with at least nine children) had been living in the same dwelling for longer than those with only five children. Moreover, the overcrowded families had last moved over seven years ago while families which were least overcrowded had last moved on average four years earlier. At the root of the problem is the fact that local housing authorities simply do not possess a sufficient number of large dwellings into which to move tenants when their families grow in size. Not only are there not enough large council dwellings but many of those which councils do possess are inadequate in other ways.

The Surroundings

Thirty-three of the families were living in flats, half of which were not on the ground floor. Living above ground level created several problems for the families. First there was the constant worry that the neighbours underneath might be disturbed by noise. Those who lived several floors up had further problems. Playing space was limited and there was the extra burden of carrying babies, shopping, fuel and washing up several flights of stone steps, for none of the blocks in which the families lived had a lift. Mrs. Cuthbert, who lived on the fourth floor, had broken down under the strain of carrying babies, shopping, washing and coal up to her flat. She reported that she had spent some time in hospital as a result. 'They told me to rest a lot when I came out—how can I when I've got three little ones at home all day. Besides my eldest boy is only eleven, he's very good and does a lot of shopping for me—he even looks around for the cheapest prices, but he shouldn't carry heavy loads up and down all those stairs.' Altogether sixteen of the families washed and dried their clothes away from their own homes because they lacked the necessary drying space and had no spin drier. All but five were flat dwellers.

Three-quarters (sixty-one) of the families were fortunate enough to have their own garden or a park nearby with no busy roads to cross, but the children of sixteen families, one-sixth (105) of the children in the survey had no garden and no park within a convenient distance to play in. A further nine families were only a little better off as they had access only to the balcony or courtyard of the block of flats in which they were living, both places where young children could soon be out of sight and more important out of 'rescuing' distance of their mothers.

It is particularly important for children living in cramped and cluttered homes to have adequate play space. However the homes of eighteen of the twenty-five families who did not have easy access to safe play space were overcrowded. Some mothers, living several floors up in a block of flats, did not dare let their children out of the flats. The balconies had walls which could be climbed. Neighbours objected to children peddling tricycles etc. up and down past their front doors. The stone steps leading to the floors below were dangerous for the younger children. Often the courtyard of the flats had easy access to a busy main road: one mother's little boy, aged six, had been knocked down by a lorry six months previously. He only broke a leg and was luckier than another little boy she had known who had been playing under a pile of leaves by the side of the road and was killed when a lorry backed into him. Most mothers felt the older children could look after themselves but they were most concerned about the younger children. The children of large families in London appear worse off than children in smaller families in this respect. As many as 18 per cent of the families had no access to a garden or yard compared with 5 per cent of the national sample of families with primary school children.[13]

13. The national sample included 3,092 families with at least one primary school child. Among children from social class V, 11 per cent had no access to a garden or yard. Children and their Primary Schools (The Plowden Report) *op. cit.*, p. 113. The differences between the large families in the London study, and the families in the national sample may in part be explained by the fact that families of all sizes in London may have less access to garden or yards compared with families living elsewhere in England.

Altogether a third (twenty-nine) of the familes were living in an environment lacking suitable play space for children or having inadequate facilities for washing and drying clothes or were living in flats which were not on the ground floor and had no lift. Thirteen of these families had a weekly income of less than £20. These families included 30 per cent of council tenants, 60 per cent of the private tenants and 20 per cent of the owner-occupiers.

Total Adequacy

Accommodation which was inadequate in one respect was likely to be inadequate in another. All but four of the forty families living in substandard housing and all but five of the sixteen families lacking play space were also overcrowded. Altogether eighteen families were below standard on all three scales. Table 3.4 shows how these are related to income.

TABLE 3.4

Number and Percentage of Families Lacking Good Standards of Accommodation, Adequate Space in the Home and an Accessible Playing Area for Children

Lacking good accommodation, space and playing area	Household Income as Per cent of National Assistance Scale		All families[1]	
	under 140	140 and over	N	%
Lacking none	6	11	20	23
lacking one	10	8	21	24
Lacking two	21	6	27	32
Lacking all three	12	6	18	21
Total	49	31	86	100

(1) Total includes six families for whom income was unknown.

The data can also be expressed from the vantage point of the children. At the time of the survey 41 per cent of the children were living in accommodation that was both overcrowded and lacking amenities. A quarter of these children (sixty-six) were living in property so lacking in amenities that it had been condemned as unfit for habitation. Although not all would spend the whole of their childhood in these houses, these results suggest that the proportion of children from large families in London who are brought up in totally inadequate dwellings is considerably higher than among smaller families in the country as a whole.[14]

The Effects of Inadequate Housing on Family Life

How did overcrowding, lack of amenities and safe play space

---

14. "Of the 5,000 children followed over eighteen years since 1946 in the National Survey of Health and Development . . . 2 per cent (lived) in homes that during the whole of their childhood were consistently overcrowded and lacked amenities." Children and their Primary Schools (The Plowden Report) *op. cit.*, Vol. 2. Appendix 2, p. 77.

affect the family? What did this mean in terms of everyday living? In what ways were the lives of the families restricted by their physical surroundings?

Overcrowding had obvious implications for the ways in which family life was organised. The mothers complained most about the difficulties of providing satisfactory sleeping arrangements and the inability of family members to carry out separate activities. These difficulties became worse as the children reached their teens and did not want to be continuously involved in the whole family's activities. The Fuller's eldest boy no longer wanted to share a bedroom with his four younger brothers: 'He's threatening to move downstairs and sleep in the front room. I can understand how he feels because now he's started work he's got a lot of his own things, but the little ones keep pulling them about. I don't know what to do—I can't let him turn my front room into a bedroom, it's the only room I can keep decent and fetch visitors into.' Mrs. Fuller's dilemma was a very real one because for her the tidy front room was one of her last symbols of respectability. Other mothers wanted two living rooms for practical reasons as well as for status. 'You never know what visitors might sit on: there's usually toys everywhere and the kids put their sticky fingers all over the place. I'd like one room to keep for best and one to really live in,' said Mrs. Downie. Mothers of teenage sons and daughters were very concerned that they should be able to bring friends home without involving them with the whole family. For many families the problems would have been considerably eased if they had had a large enough kitchen to eat in but nearly half the families (forty) had only small kitchens. Similarly problems would have been eased if the flat or house had more bedrooms. Altogether fourteen families wanted at least one more bedroom.

On the other hand there were parents who obviously enjoyed their very close family life and expected their visitors to do the same. Given another room some families would not or could not have used it. 'We only want one living room, because we couldn't live in two—one of them would be shut off all the time,' explained Mrs. Golding. However, the way in which the families used their accommodation was governed not only by the space available but also whether they could afford to furnish and heat several rooms adequately. The really poor families could barely afford to heat and furnish the accommodation they already had. The mothers managed without a fire all day. They lit it in time for when the children came home from school and even then there were occasions when the whole family went to bed in the evening to keep warm. Altogether fifteen families only ever heated one living room. Mrs. Clifford for example, was interviewed in her big kitchen. Here she sat with all the family: the baby asleep in the pram, another on her knee and the other six watching the television. This was the room where they all ate, where the children played, washed and got ready for bed. They had another large sitting room which was cold and cheerless in comparison with the warm, lively kitchen. 'We use it only at Christmas and for birthdays—it takes so much to heat it. I've been trying to get an exchange for ages, somewhere with smaller rooms. People come and look at the flat but when they see the huge rooms they lose interest.'

Life for the parents and children of the wealthier families was so much easier: they did not have accommodation problems of the same kind. These families had sufficient room for their needs and enough bedrooms for the children to have their friends to stay in the holidays. One family had added an annexe to the house when the children grew older so that the boys had rooms of their own where they could do their homework. There were enough built-in cupboards for all the children to keep their belongings safely stored away from the little ones. Their homes and gardens for the children to play in and the houses were spaced far enough apart for the neighbours not to be disturbed by noise.

Attempts to find better Accommodation

Less than one-third (twenty-four) of the families were satisfied with their accommodation. This included nearly two-thirds of the owner-occupiers, and a fifth of the council and private tenants. The majority of the families found their accommodation lacking in one or more respects, although only ten thought they were experiencing their worst housing problems at the time of the survey. Three of these families were living in rented accommodation and were still on the housing list.

An extreme example were Mr. and Mrs. Caulder who had been homeless twice, once for eighteen months, and once for six months. They had then moved to Scotland to try and find accommodation and work. Although they found somewhere to live, there were few job opportunities for Mr. Caulder so after a year, they moved back to the same borough. Later four of their children were taken into care for four years because they were still unable to find adequate accommodation. By the time of the survey the family had been reunited again and living in three rooms of Mrs. Caulder's mother's terraced house. Mr. and Mrs. Caulder were sleeping in the kitchen. They had been on the housing list for two years, because while living away from the borough they had lost their previous place on the list. Mrs. Caulder was very bitter about this, especially as she had lived in the borough all her life, apart from that one year in Scotland. She had almost given up all hopes of ever getting housed.

She no longer wrote to or visited the housing department because she did not know what else to do to convince them of her need for a house: she had experienced homelessness, her family had been split up and meanwhile she was enduring chronic overcrowding. Her attitude seemed not one of apathy—but of despair.

Council tenants also experienced delays and despair. The majority of them were living in accommodation that was not only overcrowded but had structural defects or lacked amenities. Only nine council tenants were completely satisfied, whereas half (twenty-nine) wanted to move and were trying to do something about it. Nine families had seen the council in the three months prior to the survey, four had asked their general practitioner or the health visitor to contact the council on their behalf and ten were waiting for an exchange or transfer. Two families had recently been offered alternative accommodation but had refused because in both cases they had been offered fourth floor flats in blocks on busy main roads. Three, like Mrs. Caulder, felt their efforts to convince the council of their need to move were useless and had given up. 'Once you are in these buildings they forget about you—they just don't want to know,' said one mother. 'They just say there's lots like you or there's families worse off than you are, you shouldn't complain,' said another. Most families were well aware that there were families worse off, after all most of them had experienced worse conditions themselves. Nevertheless, they also knew a lot of families were *better* off.

The families also found it difficult to get any information from the housing department, about the likelihood of being rehoused. Letters received no reply and many of the mothers had little time or were reluctant actually to visit the housing department. One family was living in an old house due for slum clearance. It was damp, the roof leaked and it needed repair and decoration. The family were reluctant to spend time and money on repairs if they were only going to be there for a short time, on the other hand the mother was worried that the dampness was affecting the health of the family. Her children had had more colds than usual in the previous winter. She herself had been ill with suspected tuberculosis (a condition her doctor felt could be attributed in part to the dampness in the house). Repeated requests to the housing department for an estimate of how long it would be before they moved met with silence. Mrs. Henry had been ill and had been unable to visit the housing department and her husband worked long hours. The only information they received came eventually from his employer. He told them the house was due to be demolished in four months time because his firm had been asked to do the demolition!

Mrs. Stanley whose appalling accommodation has already been

described[15] explained how she continued her battle with the council to get them to find her alternative accommodation. 'I write to the housing manager every week, but it's no use—you can't win at the council. The inspector of health came round once and said it should be condemned. He noticed how badly the fire smoked "detrimental to health" he said. He asked about the rats in the cellar too. Even the Assistance Board think it terrible.' Although the National Assistance Board were aware of the condition of her accommodation they could not allow her to protest by witholding her rent. At one time Mrs. Stanley refused to pay the rent for ten weeks, hoping this would draw attention to her situation. The Assistance Board, however, insisted that she paid it and that if she did not, the Board would pay it direct to the council. It was not surprising that families in these circumstances felt that they were put in old, substandard property and conveniently overlooked because their needs were different from those of the average family. As Mrs. Stanley said in desperation, 'I've done a wicked thing and had a large family.'[16]

Expenditure on Housing

TABLE 3.5

Expenditure on Housing by Families with Different Weekly Income

| Housing costs | Household Income | | | Mean |
	Under £20	£20 and less than £30	£30 and over	
Council Tenants	19	25	8	52
Mean Rent (shillings)	62/7	66/6	57/9	61/–
Rent as proportion of income	18%	13%	8%	14%
Private Tenants	2	7	1	10
Mean Rent (shillings)	31/–	72/6	64/6	57/–
Rent as proportion of income	9%	16%	10%	14%
Owner-Occupiers	1	5	12	18
Mean housing cost (shillings)	59/–	68/3	125/–	98/9
Housing cost as proportion of income	16%	14%	14%	14%

Expenditure on housing was a major item in the household budget for many families. Fifteen families spent more than one fifth of their income on accommodation and only thirteen spent the same proportion (10.3 per cent) or less than the average two-child family.[17] Ten

---

15. See p. 33.
16. The families may not have been entirely wrong in assuming that local housing authorities may equate large families with problem families. For example the G.L.C. Housing Committee at a meeting on 11th May 1967 recommended an increase in the number of enforced transfers from high density accommodation as 'a valuable disciplinary measure' to deal with hooliganism. 'To enable this to be done the Committee has authorised an increase over the next year from 50 to 75 in the number of individual houses that may be acquired by agreement for rehousing *large or difficult families*.' Minutes of G.L.C. Council Meeting 6th/7th June 1967, p. 353 (Author's italics).
17. Mean housing costs for a family with two children in 1965 were 48/6. Ministry of Labour *Family Expenditure Survey Report for 1965*, London, H.M.S.O., 1966, p. 84, Table 13.

of the latter families were in the top income group. In the private market the proportion of the households income spent on housing did not differ greatly between income groups. Among council tenants if differential rent schemes and rent rebates were effective, a similar pattern would be expected. However this was not the case because the average rent paid varied little between income groups and although there was some variation within each income group, the extent of the variation was similar.

Only five council tenants were paying reduced rents: although a total of forty-eight families were living in accommodation owned by a housing authority which operated a rent rebate or differential rent scheme, only one of these families belonged to the group of sixteen whose incomes were below basic National Assistance level, whereas three had a weekly income of over £25. This can partly be explained by the fact that nine of the families in the lowest income group were recipients of National Assistance and some housing authorities expect that the rent will be paid in full in such circumstances. Mr. Bromley for example, had been paying a reduced rent to one of the London boroughs before he became unemployed but when he started drawing National Assistance the council removed the rebate on the grounds that they were not going to subsidise the National Assistance Board. However, the National Assistance Board took the view that they could not pay more than Mr. Bromley's normal earnings, even if his rent increased. Thus Mr. Bromley had to pay the whole rent himself. The Greater London Council accept that the full rent rebate should go to a family subject to the wage stop, so the two families drawing National Assistance and living in property owned by this authority continued to receive their rebate. Altogether seven of the sixteen council tenants whose incomes were below basic National Assistance level were paying more than a fifth of their income on rent. Three of the families were paying over seventy shillings a week. However only two families would have had an income adequate for the rest of their needs[18] if they had paid no more than forty shillings (10 per cent of their income) in rent. For the remaining sixteen families, low basic wages or inadequate state benefits, not high rents were the primary cause of their inadequate incomes.

Over one third (twenty) of the council tenants had had difficulty in paying a rent which took no account of their inadequate income and as a result had either been in rent arrears in the previous three months or were in arrears at the time of the survey. None of the families in arrears had incomes above 140 per cent of the basic National Assistance level and over half (eleven) had incomes below

18. Adequacy measured by comparing the household income less housing costs with total National Assistance basic allowances payable to that household *before* adding housing costs.

basic National Assistance level. None were receiving a rent rebate. Altogether nearly two-thirds of council tenants with an income below basic National Assistance level had experienced difficulties in maintaining their rent payments.

The lack of relationship between rents paid and household income could not be explained by differences in the size of dwelling occupied by the families. Those with four bedrooms (excluding kitchen and bathroom) paid an average of fifty-eight shillings a week, those with five rooms, sixty-three shillings, and those with six rooms or more sixty-four shillings. There was little difference between the rents paid by families living in substandard accommodation and those living in satisfactory dwellings. The families living in condemned property were paying on average fifty-eight shillings a week and those below the 12-point scale sixty-one shillings on average. This compares with an average rent of sixty shillings for all families living in rented accommodation and an average seventy-nine shillings housing costs for the whole sample.

Conclusions

The relationship between the adequacy and condition of a family's dwelling and its income is not straight forward. Whereas it is true that the low wage earner's family, whether large or small, lives in the worst housing in the private market,[19] the results of this survey suggest that the standard of a council tenant's accommodation depends less on family income and more on family size. Irrespective of their income the families with more than an average number of children live in worse conditions than families with only two or three children.

---

19. Housing in Greater London (The Milner Holland Report) *op. cit.* pp. 91–94.

4. HOUSEKEEPING FOR A LARGE FAMILY

We showed in Chapter 2 that the sources and levels of income of these families varied considerably. In this chapter we examine how the families spent their money and show the ways in which low incomes prohibit or at least restrict spending on certain items and determine the method by which particular items are bought. The limitations placed on spending were not necessarily felt equally by all members of the family and the mothers told us how the need for economy affected some members of the family more than the others.

The collection of detailed and accurate expenditure information is difficult, and a single interview is certainly not the best method for attempting to achieve it.[1] In view of the amount of information sought on other topics, it was impractical to ask the mother to embark upon the time-consuming exercise of recalling all her expenditure. Instead questions were restricted to expenditure on particular items of food: milk, bread, potatoes, fresh fruit and meat, together with a rough estimate of total food expenditure. It was also possible to obtain particulars of such regular payments as clothing clubs, hire purchase and fuel as these were easy to remember. Methods of buying household items varied between income groups and these variations indicated as much about the restrictions on choice as do the actual proportions of income spent on them.

Food

Without a full nutritional analysis of the food bought, methods of preparation and variable consumption within the family, it is impossible to assess the full nutritional implications of variation in diet. This analysis is therefore limited in range. But in relation to income there were some important findings. Certain types of food

---

1. The Government Social Survey requires the families in their expenditure studies to keep very detailed diaries of every item of expenditure (amounting to about 100 separate items) for two weeks. Some market research experts maintain that many families overestimate their expenditure for a period of at least six weeks, so for a true picture of expenditure diaries should be kept for a minimum of two months. Certainly there are large discrepancies between income and recorded expenditure in the Family Expenditure Survey. For a further discussion see Abel-Smith, B. Townsend, P. *The Poor and the Poorest*, Occasional Papers on Social Administration No. 17, G. Bell and Sons, Ltd., London, 1965, Appendix II.

no longer appeared on the menu of families with low incomes. Cheap starchy food was substituted. This was an expected finding, for it is well established that large families eat more bread and potatoes and less meat, fish, butter, fresh vegetables and fruit than smaller families.[2] It was not until the weekly family income was above 140 per cent of basic National Assistance level that the consumption of these foodstuffs per capita in the majority of the large families approached the mean per capita for the United Kingdom.[3] Fruit was one of the first items to be dropped from the family's menu and nearly half (forty) the families purchased fruit seldom or not at all. Milk consumption also declined as income fell. Whereas only four families with an income above 140 per cent of basic National Assistance level drank less milk per capita than the mean for the United Kingdom the proportion among those whose incomes were below the basic National Assistance level was much higher: nearly three-quarters (thirteen families). The figures (Table 4.1) indicate that the consumption of carbohydrates in the form of bread and potatoes increases as income declines. The difference between income groups are less marked, perhaps because it was not possible to take into account variations in the age and sex of the children in each family. It seems reasonable to suppose that a family with three or four teenage sons is more likely to consume more carbohydrates than one with teenage daughters.

TABLE 4.1

Number and Percentage of Families with Different Income who Consume Above the Average bread and potatoes and below the average milk and fruit

Items consumed	Household Income as per cent of National Assistance Scale						All families[1]	
	under 100		100 but less than 140		140 and over			
	N	%	N	%	N	%	N	%
Bread above average	5	(28)	11	(35)	6	(19)	23	27
Potatoes above average	10	(55)	13	(42)	12	(39)	37	43
Milk below average	13	(72)	17	(55)	4	(13)	35	41
Fruit never or seldom	14	(78)	15	(48)	10	(32)	40	46
Total	18	(100)	31	(100)	31	(100)	86	100

(1) All families include six whose income was unknown.

These figures, however, do not show some of the extreme variations in consumption. For example, each of two families (one with fourteen children, the other with ten) ate each week 100 pounds of potatoes,

---

2. Ministry of Agriculture, Fisheries and Food. *Domestic Food Consumption and Expenditure 1963* National Food Survey Committee, London, H.M.S.O. 1965, p. 25.
3. In 1964 the mean weekly consumption/person in the United Kingdom:
   of milk was   4·8 pints
   of bread was   3 lbs.
   of potatoes was 4 lbs.
   Ministry of Agriculture, Fisheries and Food, *op. cit.*, pp. 63–65, Table 24.

together with more than twenty large loaves of bread. Five families had less than three pints of milk each per week but eleven had more than twice this amount. 'We need a cow in this house,' said Mrs. Trollope, whose family of ten children drank ten and a half gallons of milk a week.

There is another, more important fact hidden by these figures. An average per person based on the family's total consumption implies that the food is divided equally among family members. The mother, however, was likely to eat less than the rest of the family when money was short. The figures of milk consumption in Table 4.1 include free welfare milk and free school milk. For twenty-one families (all with incomes below £25) free milk accounted for over a third of their total milk consumption. Most of this was drunk by the children, so the per capita consumption of their parents was less. During school holidays the children's milk consumption dropped in all but five families in this group who bought extra milk because their children were not getting their free school milk.

To discover how far their diet was restricted for financial reasons as distinct from cultural ones, the mother was asked what she would buy more of if she had more money to spend on food. Table 4.2 summarizes the results. Only a quarter of the families were completely satisfied with their diet and, as the Table 4.2 shows, the majority of these were in the top income group. All the families in the bottom income group would have liked more money to spend on food, particularly meat and fresh fruit.

TABLE 4.2

Number and Percentage of Families with Different Incomes who Desire Extra Food

Items on which family would spend extra money, if any	Household Income as per cent of National Assistance Scale							
	under 100		100 but less than 140		140 and over		All families[1]	
	N	%	N	%	N	%	N	%
Meat	13	(72)	17	(55)	11	(35)	43	50
Fruit	11	(61)	12	(39)	10	(32)	34	40
Biscuits, Cake	4	(22)	6	(19)	4	(13)	16	18
Puddings	3	(17)	3	(10)	–	–	7	9
Eggs	2	(11)	2	(6)	4	(13)	8	9
None	–	–	5	(16)	13	(42)	20	22
Total	18	(100)	31	(100)	31	(100)	86	100

(1) All families includes six families whose income was unknown.

The most common complaint made by the poorer families about their diet was the lack of variety. Food was a conscious expression of indulgence in some families. 'Food makes up for our not going out,' said one mother and 'Food is our only luxury,' said another.

Some mothers would talk of wanting to buy 'luscious cake' or to make a fancy pudding. 'Afters' became a weekly treat or disappeared altogether, in the poorer families. Those who wished they had more money to spend on meat, not only wanted to buy larger quantities but wanted to have dearer cuts instead of the mincemeat or sausages they had to buy if the whole family was to share the meal. Twelve specifically mentioned wanting chicken, for with their large families they would need at least two if everyone was to have a presentable helping.

Children in the poorer families often had a very limited diet because they were not encouraged to try and eat new foods. This happened partly out of necessity: a mother who cannot afford to waste food is less likely to experiment with unfamiliar foods and more likely to provide the well-known favourites. Apart from potatoes, tinned peas were the commonest vegetable eaten among the poorer families because some of the children did not like 'greens'. Three of the nine families who never bought fruit explained that the children would not eat it if given the chance; they therefore preferred to buy something which they were sure the children would eat. However, these families were exceptions, for, as Table 4.2 shows, apart from meat, the families said they felt the lack of fruit the most.[4]

There was one item of food, however, that had considerable psychological significance for the poorer family. A family who entirely substituted margarine for butter had admitted to themselves that they were poor, so big efforts were made to go on buying butter. 'Poor as I am, not a scrap of marge comes into this house,' said Mrs. Johnson, for example. Only one of the families in the lowest income group had changed entirely to margarine and as she said, 'You *can* tell Stork from butter.'

Meal Patterns

There were major variations in meal patterns between income groups. Where the income was high, the whole family ate the same meals, usually together. However, as the household income dropped and with it the amount of money available for food, the mother could no longer afford to provide substantial meals for the whole family.

The difference between rich and poor families was shown by the extent to which the father was joined in his evening meal by other members of the family. In the higher income families he was very likely to be joined by the whole family, excluding perhaps the

---

4. This is a much higher proportion than among a sample of smaller families who were asked the same question. Only 28 per cent said they would buy extra fruit, compared with 40 per cent of the large families. The proportion wanting to buy more meat was, however, almost the same (51 per cent). McKenzie J., *Poverty: Food and Nutrition Indices.* Office of Health Economics, London 1967.
    (It could be that the mothers of the larger families interviewed said they would buy more fruit if they could because they thought it was the answer expected of them.)

youngest children who would have eaten earlier. A total of twenty-seven families ate an evening meal together but this included half of those with weekly incomes over £30 and only a quarter of those with weekly incomes under £20. By contrast, the twenty-two families in which the father received preferential treatment and was the only member of the family to have a cooked evening meal, apart from earning children, only one had an income above £30 but over half (fifteen) had incomes under £25.

Breakfasts followed a similar pattern. Twenty-three fathers had a cooked breakfast, of bacon and egg, but they were joined by the whole family in only seven households and by the children in only five. The lower the income, the more likely it was both father and children had only cereal or toast. Among the forty-four families with weekly incomes under £25, only four gave the children and only three gave the father, a cooked breakfast.

However restricted the meals eaten during the week, a major effort was made to provide a 'Sunday dinner' such as was enjoyed by other families. A family unable to have a Sunday joint with the accompanying vegetables, and a pudding to follow felt very poor. Even if the mother could only afford to spend six or seven shillings on meat she would spend it on a joint (this to be divided between at least seven people, for which the richer families paid £2 or £3) rather than buy for example double the quantity of mincemeat. One family could only afford a joint when it was not rent week (many council rents are paid fortnightly) and four more did not always have a joint in the school holidays, when, without a free school meal in the middle of the day, the mother felt obliged to purchase more than bread and jam for tea.

The major variations in meal patterns between members of the family show how economy measures affected some members of the family more than others. At every meal, it was the mother who suffered the severest restriction when income was low. One reason for this was that she was the one, apart from the children under school age, most dependent on meals provided at home. Altogether 78 per cent of the school children had a midday meal at school and over half (fifty-two) of the fathers who did not come home in the middle of the day had a hot meal in the canteen at work or in a nearby cafe. Forty-three mothers only had a sandwich in the middle of the day and a further four had nothing except a cup of tea. This was not because they had had a large breakfast: more than twenty-one mothers ate nothing for breakfast and nothing more than a sandwich for lunch. Although twenty-three fathers also ate sandwiches for lunch, seven had had a cooked breakfast and six had had nothing. Seven mothers never had a hot cooked meal: they existed on tea, bread and jam or chips and sometimes cigarettes.

'I don't bother about myself—I don't really feel hungry often. It's the nippers who need food to build them up,' explained one of the mothers.

Nevertheless, various devices were used to limit the amount of food the children asked for. For example, one mother no longer gave her children tea as soon as they came home from school; instead they had to wait an hour so that they could not feel hungry again before they went to bed. Another bought peanut butter instead of jam because it lasted longer as the children did not like it so much. Three families were so poor that even the father did not have a hot meal in the evenings. The whole family had either a sandwich or bread-and-butter and jam.

Clothing

Another effect of low income was reliance on second-hand clothing or special clothing grants from the education department, the welfare department or the National Assistance Board. The richest families paid cash for clothing when they needed it, the majority of middle income families could not afford to pay cash when buying new clothing and so bought some, if not all of their clothing on credit through clothing clubs or Provident checks.[5] The poorer families in turn, could not afford to buy on credit and depended on jumble sales, gifts from family, friends and welfare organisations (see Table 4.3).

TABLE 4.3
*Number and Percentage of Families with Different Incomes
who Bought Second-Hand Clothing*

Major source of clothing	Household Income as per cent of National Assistance Scale						All families[1]	
	under 100		100 but less than 140		140 and over			
	N	%	N	%	N	%	N	%
New								
Cash	1	(6)	8	(28)	19	(62)	30	35
Credit	6	(33)	14	(44)	10	(32)	33	39
Second-hand								
Cash	5	(28)	7	(22)	–	–	12	14
Gifts	6	(33)	2	(6)	2	(6)	11	12
Total	18	(100)	31	(100)	31	(100)	86	100

(1) All families includes six families for whom income was unknown.

All but two of the mothers who bought clothing on credit thought they paid more for clothing which was often (although not always)

5. Anyone who pays £1 for a Provident check can go to a shop which belongs to the scheme and get up to £10 worth of clothing. This is paid back weekly over a certain period of time, and an extra 1s. in every £1 is charged for this credit. To belong to the scheme a shop may have to pay between 12 per cent – 15 per cent of the value of the sales made in this way.

of poorer quality. 'It's the biggest robbery in the world—you only get rubbish. They make money out of the likes of us,' complained one mother when she was asked whether she thought clothing bought on credit was good value.

Altogether, fifteen mothers went to jumble sales to buy some if not most of their clothing and two more went to second-hand clothes shops as they disliked the roughness of the jumble sales. There were two reactions to buying second-hand clothing. Some enjoyed going to jumble sales and went as much for pleasure as for clothes. As one mother said, 'You get stupendous bargains—I even bought a chair for half-a-crown last time. It was raining so I carried it back over my head. I never used to buy shoes but now I sometimes get sandals, but I clean them out with Dettol before the children wear them.' Other mothers did not like buying second-hand clothing unless they knew who had worn them before and would not do so unless it was absolutely necessary.

Shoes

Children's shoes were a constant worry to many families. The poorer mothers felt they had little choice of how or when to buy them. If three children all needed shoes at the same time and there was no spare housekeeping, certainly not as much as £6 or £7, then they either had to borrow money, buy on credit or get assistance from the education or welfare department. Most bought on credit in these circumstances, although they were aware that this was an unsatisfactory solution because the shoes they bought were often of poor quality and wore out quickly. As the mother of six boys explained: 'That's my worst problem—shoes. I don't like the tally-man for shoes. I paid him 43s for the last pair and they didn't last as well as those bought at the shop. David (aged 12) has gone through three pairs in four months—the uppers come apart each time and it's useless trying to have them mended.'

During the six months preceding the survey nine families had been unable to buy on credit and eventually, when the children missed school through having no shoes to wear, the school care committee had provided shoes for them.

Both the mother and the father felt the restrictions of a limited income when it came to buying clothing for themselves. The fathers were responsible for buying their own clothing in three-quarters (sixty-two) of the families. Occasionally they were supplied with shoes and a uniform at work.[6] It was at least four years since most (fourteen) of the fathers (eighteen) in the lowest income group had had a new suit or jacket.

---

6. Unfortunately, information on clothing provided at work was not collected consistently.

Eleven[7] mothers had not had a new coat or dress since their marriage. Half of them came from families in which the weekly income was less than £20. In contrast, the mothers of the families in the top income group had new outfits annually. Obtaining shoes for themselves was also a problem for the poorer mothers. Mrs. Bromley was wearing an odd pair of shoes when she was interviewed for she did not have a matching pair. Another mother only had a pair of slippers and could not go out when it was raining, and one mother explained that she had just had to treat herself to a new pair of shoes from the tally man three weeks previously because she did not have any in which to go outdoors.

Fuel and Light

Keeping warm was a constant problem for the poorer families, made worse in some families by inadequate food and clothing. The form of fuel used for heating the home depended on the family's income. Two-thirds of the families with an income of £35 or more chose methods which involved the least amount of work. They relied entirely on central heating or gas and electric fires. In contrast all except two of the families with weekly incomes under £20 used solid fuel as their main form of heating. Half of the families in this group had no other form of heating. The middle income families also relied on solid fuel but used other forms of heating to supplement it. Altogether, twenty families used paraffin heaters when it was very cold to warm the bedrooms or provide extra heat in the living room. The majority (three-quarters) of paraffin users were in the middle income range. Only one relied on paraffin heating entirely. Occasionally families were able to find wood to burn on the fire. For example, Mrs. Oliver's fourteen-year-old son collected old packing boxes and crates from the greengrocer at weekends when it was really cold.

The poorer families limited the amount they spent on heating, not by using cheaper substitutes for coal, gas or electricity, but by buying less coal altogether. One family who, after paying the rent, had £11 a week on which to feed, clothe and care for six children, reported going to bed in the winter to keep warm. They could only afford one bag of coal (costing 5s 6d) a day and when it was very cold this was not sufficient.

Methods of paying for fuel and light depended also on the income of the family. The high income families paid their bills quarterly. The low income families had slot meters for both gas and electricity and in order to ration coal they bought it daily or sometimes

---

7. This is probably an underestimate because it was not until several families had been interviewed that it became clear that the mothers' inability to buy new clothing for herself was an indication of a very inadequate income.

weekly. Other families spread the cost by paying 12s, say, weekly all the year round, although they only used coal in the winter months.

Slot meters had a number of advantages for these families. In the first place they were a method of forced saving and the quarterly rebate received could amount to £6 or £7 in the winter months. Sometimes this money was put straight back into the meter, sometimes it covered the quarterly payments on the heater, washing machine or refrigerator. It was spent on whatever was urgently needed at the time. Mrs. Bromley was so short of money that when asked what the rebate was spent on replied, 'I go straight out and buy a dinner.' Secondly, by paying for gas or electricity as they used it the family could avoid the danger of not saving enough money to pay a big bill. Four families had changed from paying for their electricity quarterly to having a slot meter because they had been unable to save sufficient money to meet a large bill. 'We had the electricity cut off for six weeks because I couldn't pay the bill. I felt like Florence Nightingale going round with lamps and candles and things. We've had a meter put in now,' explained Mrs. O'Malley who had recently moved from a one-room flat to a four-bedroom council house and was only just beginning to adjust to the big increase in household costs.

A further advantage of a slot meter was that it was a method of paying which could be shared among other members of the family. The change from paying quarterly bills to paying into a meter transfers responsibility for payment from father to mother. However, responsibility wasn't transferred completely, because fathers were expected to contribute when necessary, or as one mother said, 'I don't have shillings when he's around—I'm not daft!' Also earning children often put money in the meter.[8]

Furniture and Appliances

The acquisition of sufficient furniture and appliances with which to run the home was a further major problem. Nearly one in four families (nineteen) were still buying basic furniture: beds, tables and chairs. Thirty-two families had an insufficient number of beds and altogether ninety-nine children (16 per cent) were sharing a bed.[9] This included 18 per cent of those under ten years old and 15 per cent of those over ten years old: higher proportions than among children of smaller families.[10] Adequate sleeping arrangements for the children depended less on space than on the family's

8. Slot T.V., (which six families had) was both a method of forced saving and of spreading the cost among all the earning members of the family. Responsibility for household payment is outlined fully, pp. 64–66.
9. Sharing a bed meant two or more children in a single bed and three or more in a double bed.
10. This is significantly higher at the one per cent level. 12 per cent of the children in the National Health and Development Survey shared a bed. Children and their Primary Schools (The Plowden Report) *op. cit.*, Vol. 2, Appendix 2, p. 77.

financial position. Bunk beds could solve the space problem to a certain extent, but providing each child with a bed or its equivalent also meant acquiring sufficient sheets and blankets. Several families were still buying bedding and some mentioned the use of coats as blankets in the winter. One enterprising mother had unpicked old coats and sewed them into blankets.

In some cases lack of furniture was a reflection of the family's housing history. Half of those still buying beds or chairs had previously been homeless or had been living in very overcrowded conditions. For example, Mrs. Finch had been living with her nine children in a one-room basement flat. She and her husband had slept on the floor on a mattress in the kitchen for six years. Apart from adjustments like getting used to sleeping in a bed again which took Mr. Finch six months, the change from these cramped conditions to an unfurnished council house meant a lot of furniture was needed suddenly. This was difficult for families without resources if friends and relatives could not rally round, especially when they had had little chance to acquire a store of furniture gradually. Even second-hand furniture was beyond the means of some families, so hire purchase was the only way to buy. Only two families with weekly incomes below £25 had hire purchase commitments for furniture other than beds, chairs or floor coverings: 'keeping up with the Jones' was a luxury the families could not afford.

Some families justified their lack of good furniture by saying that with several young children there was little point in buying good quality furniture because it would get ruined just the same. As one mother said, 'We wouldn't buy a "home" until the children grew up, a decent "home" has got to last.'

TABLE 4.4

The Number and Percentage of Families with Different Incomes who had Certain Consumer Durables

Consumer Durables	Household Income as per cent of National Assistance Scale						All Families in Sample[1]		All Households in Greater London Conurbation[2]
	under 100		100 but less than 140		140 and over				
	N	%	N	%	N	%	N	%	%
Television	18	(100)	31	(100)	31	(100)	86	100	78
Refrigerator	4	(22)	17	(55)	28	(90)	52	60	56
Washing machine	1	(6)	12	(39)	16	(52)	34	39	41
Telephone	–	–	4	(13)	12	(39)	17	20	39
Car	1	(6)	2	(6)	10	(32)	12	14	37
All five	–	–	1	(3)	8	(26)	9	10	(not stated)
Total	18	(100)	31	(100)	31	(100)	86	100	100

(1) All families include six whose income was not known.
(2) Source: Ministry of Labour *Family Expenditure Survey, Report for 1964,* London, H.M.S.O. 1965, p. 28, Table V.

Only one family had been married less than ten years. Nevertheless, many still lacked basic furniture and equipment and some were still in the process of buying it. All the families had the use of a gas or electric cooker but thirteen families were still paying the hire purchase instalments and a further seven were renting one. Four of these families had an income below the basic national assistance level and only two were in the top income group. The proportion of families with a washing machine was slightly lower than the proportion for all London households even though those who had them considered them essential for a large household. Half of the families without one, however, said they would buy one next if they had the money. In considering the figures for the large familes and all London households in Table 4.4 it should of course be remembered that the latter include large proportions of pensioner and single person households. The usefulness of a refrigerator depended on the family's income. Altogether, six families were buying a refrigerator on hire purchase and four were renting one. None of these families were in the highest income group in which, as Table 4.4 shows, all but three owned a refrigerator.

Expenditure on Furniture and Consumer Durables

The families with incomes below the basic National Assistance level were spending on average 8 per cent of their income on hire purchase instalments or rentals. The middle and higher income groups spent smaller proportions: 4 per cent and 2 per cent respectively. It is cheaper to buy a large item such as a cooker outright but the poorer families could not build up sufficient resources to pay for a large item. Hire purchase was the only way they felt able to have this basic equipment. As one mother said, 'Without H.P. I wouldn't even have a mop. Still, we only buy one thing at a time. We don't go too high.'

Few of the very poor families could even do this and if gifts from friends or relatives were not forthcoming they went without. Most did go without as is shown in Table 4.4. Only two families had been given a second-hand washing machine and only one a refrigerator.

Treats and Extras

The discussion so far has been concerned with necessities and the extent to which the family as a whole as well as individual members limited expenditure on these basic items. But all the families spent money on items which could not be considered essential in the physiological sense. For example, every family however poor had a television set; many indulged in little treats, some regularly and others only occasionally. The reasons given by the families for expenditures of this kind show that they regarded them as necessities.

They were, moreover, responding to the pressures of living in a society in which they were relatively underprivileged.

The proportion of large families spending money on cigarettes and tobacco was not significantly different than for ordinary households. Three-quarters (sixty-five) families spent money on tobacco or cigarettes.[11] The amount they spent, on average, was 17s. The mean expenditure recorded for married couples with two children was significantly more: 23s in 1965.[12] In this study only families with a weekly income over 140 per cent of basic National Assistance level spent as much as this on average. The poorest families spent half this amount (11s on average). Several of the families said they were smoking less than a year ago or had given up. However, nine families said they (in all but two instances the mother) were smoking more. They said that this was because of the ever increasing worries or because they thought it reduced their appetite. The mean amount the father of the large families spent on smoking (13s 6d) was less than the mother (16s 6d). The proportion of fathers who smoked was much higher however, 62 per cent, compared with 44 per cent.

A much lower proportion (40 per cent) of large families than households in general spent money on betting.[13] Football pools, bingo, dogs and horse racing were the most frequently mentioned. In four families the eldest boy gave his mother a night out by paying for her to go to bingo. One mother was very successful and her living room had her winnings, blankets, sheets, knick-knacks of various kinds, stacked on the sideboard. The blankets were useful and sometimes she was able to sell some of the other items. Mrs. Cudgen, whose father was a bookie's runner, said she often won on the horses, so much so that she never worried about extra bills. The occasional win enabled them to pay the television licence (a big problem for some of the poorer families), buy a vital item of school uniform, pay off an outstanding debt, or have a little spending spree. The amounts spent on betting were small: 8s 6d a week on average for the families who said they spent money on some form of betting. Only three families spent more than 20s a week and they all had incomes above 140 per cent of basic National Assistance level. For the poorer families betting could be taken as a painless, if rather inefficient way of producing large sums of capital which the mother

11. The proportion of households recording expenditure on tobacco, cigarettes or cigars was 72 per cent in 1965. Ministry of Labour *Family Expenditure Survey, Report for 1965*, London, H.M.S.O. 1966, Appendix IV, p. 113.
12. *Ibid.*, p. 86, Table 12.
   It is known that expenditure on tobacco is under-recorded in the Family Expenditure Survey. The degree of under-recording may not differ according to the size of the family. It is possible that the expenditure recorded by large families is under-recorded less as they have to ration themselves.
13. 75 per cent of households consisting of two or more members gambled monthly or more often in one or more forms, i.e. football pools, dogs, horses, bingo. Davies, B. and Stone, P. Unpublished pilot study of social and economic effects of gambling.
   As with smoking, figures on gambling are known to be understated. There seems to be no reason to suppose the understatement is greater in large families.

could not have otherwise managed to save. Winning on the pools or 'coming up' on the horses was their only hope of escaping from perpetual pinching and scraping.

There were other 'extras' the parents of large families were well aware other people enjoyed regularly. For example, the items on which most mothers would like to have been able to spend more money were clothes, especially underclothing and stockings, make-up, jewellery, a handbag and a visit to the hairdressers. Where the family income was below £22 the mother never had money to spend on these items. They may not be considered necessary in the sense that they suffered any physical deprivation without them, but the mothers did want to be able to feel smart like other women. As Mrs. Green, the mother of seven, explained: 'Look at me, you wouldn't think I was only thirty-five would you? I know I look ten years older—my hair grey (the ribbon I'm wearing belongs to Anne) —my figure's gone, the skirt I'm wearing is five years old and I've forgotten how long I've had this jumper. They're worried about my varicose veins but I can't rest up and I know I shouldn't wear slippers so much. I just don't look at myself any more.'

The importance to the mother of having to go without new clothing can be judged by the fact that questions concerning new clothing—when did she last have a new coat or a new pair of shoes? —were the most sensitive questions on the questionnaire for the poorer families. This was not because they resented having to put the children first: comments such as 'I've left myself right undone for the children' or 'I never look at myself—I can't remember when I bought a new coat', were made sadly but not bitterly.

The father who had had to give up the regular pint of beer, a flutter on the horses or the pools found it difficult to give up these pleasures completely and occasionally spent a little on these 'non-essentials'. 'I used to go to football matches, go to the pub and play darts, have a go on the pools. I've had to give it all up, I can't even afford to do the pools—we have a bob's worth every now and again but we used to do them regular,' said Mr. Carstairs, who had chronic bronchitis and was unable to work.

Children's Pocket Money

The children also wanted money to spend on sweets, comics and little toys—all items which were not strictly necessary but which they expected to have because most of their friends had them. As one mother explained, 'I can't give them money every week—I just haven't got it. But when I do have a little extra I give it them. They think it funny when they see other children with two bob while they go without.'

Nearly a quarter of the school children went without pocket money and a further 8 per cent would not have had any if they had not earned it themselves. It is shown in Table 4.6 that the poorer children were the most likely to have no money to spend on themselves. Nearly half of these children compared with only a fifth of the children in the top income group were not given any pocket money. Parents but not other relatives or friends were the major sources of pocket money. The extent to which the responsibility for giving pocket money was shared between mother and father depended on the family's income. It was more likely to be the mother's responsibility alone among the poorer familes, just as financial responsibilities in general were hers.

TABLE 4.6

Percentage of School Children in Families with Different Incomes According to Source of Pocket Money

Source of Pocket Money	Household Income as per cent of National Assistance Scale				All School Children	
	under 100 %	100 but less than 140 %	140 and over %	Unknown %	%	N
None	37	21	15	(28)	23	91
Mother only	31	40	37	(33)	37	147
Father only	6	4	26	(20)	12	50
Both Parents	14	21	17	(14)	17	70
Relative or Friend	3	3	–	–	3	7
Child's Earnings	9	11	5	(5)	8	32
Total	100 86	100 147	100 143	100 21	100	397

The amount of pocket money given to the children also varied between income groups. Teenage children in the lowest income groups were given less than two shillings a week on average. In the top income group even primary school children received more than this and their teenage brothers and sisters received seven shillings a week on average. In addition, the mothers in the richer families were more likely to buy sweets and comics and share them among the whole family. The poorer children, however, either had to buy them themselves or had to rely on gifts from neighbours. Twelve families were given comics by the neighbours every week. Altogether fifteen families never bought comics or even newspapers regularly. They included ten families with incomes below the basic national assistance level and five with incomes up to 20 per cent above. To make up for the lack of a regular supply of comics and little toys the mother tried very hard to make birthdays a day of special treats. However, even this was difficult, especially for the older children. They invariably needed some item of clothing and were given this as a present.

Budgeting on a Low Income

'Some people do need guidance on how to spend money. I mean they abuse the money they've got. They say they're poor and yet they go on smoking and have a television,' commented the estate agent's wife who had six children and a very adequate income (£50 a week) on which to maintain the family. She was voicing a widely held view: that many people would not be poor if only they spent their money entirely on necessities. Poverty for these families is the result of mis-management rather than low income. Was there any truth in this for any of the large families in this study? This chapter has shown that many poor families smoke, have an occasional bet or give their children pocket money to spend on sweets or comics just like other families. As a result they had less money to spend on items considered more necessary. Nevertheless, the families themselves felt they were essential because of, rather than in spite of, their low income.

The mother of the poorer families did exercise considerable restraint in spending money. What seemed like thrift among the better-off families was often the effect of having more money. One of the most important restrictions a low income placed on the poorer families was that they could not take advantage of economies of scale. They had to buy food, clothing and fuel 'little and often' which, while rationing the consumption of these items, was an expensive method of buying.

The mothers not only had little choice of how they bought food or clothing, they also had little control over the timing of such purchases. They were caught up in a daily or weekly cycle. For example, the poorer mothers bought much of their food daily: they had less milk from the milkman and instead bought it daily from the local shop to avoid big weekly bills; they sent the children to the supermarket after school (many mothers commented proudly that their children knew how to 'shop around' for the best bargains). Even so, some did not avoid being short on Thursdays when the family allowance ran out and it was not yet pay day. 'Thursdays are sometimes dreadful—we even run out of tea and sugar,' explained Mr. Langley, the father of eight children who was a lorry driver and earned only £12 a week.

Family allowances played a vital part in the weekly cycle of the poorer families. There is no doubt that the fact they are paid on a Tuesday was important for it ensured that there was some money after the weekend to feed the family in the middle of the week until the next payday. 'Sometimes in the winter we'd have literally starved without them,' said Mrs. Rhodes, whose husband was a scrap dealer and had a very irregular income in the cold, snowy weather.

All except six families with weekly incomes under £25 collected their family allowances every Tuesday and altogether three-quarters of these mothers said they spent the money on food. Nine mothers used the allowances to pay the rent and the remaining six spent them on clothing. Only one father actually collected the family allowance for most considered it was given to the mother to spend for the benefit of the children.

To the higher income families these allowances were almost superflous: they were a small addition to the budget the family could easily do without. Only half of the mothers in the highest income group collected their allowances weekly, and all but one of the remaining mothers saved them until sufficient had accumulated to buy a large item of clothing for one of the children. Some of these mothers said that they did not need them, although they recognized that to those families less fortunate than themselves family allowances were probably important.

One of the worst aspects of a low income was the lack of reserves. There was nothing to fall back on in an emergency, nothing to tide them over a crisis period. The poorer families were perpetually on the edge of a crisis. It might be a weekly one: having no money to buy food on a Thursday, for example. Or it could be one they had expected: a notice to quit because they were too far in arrears with their rent, or the arrival of an electricity bill they could not pay because they had had to 'borrow' from the money put by to pay it. For some families a crisis could occur when the mother lost her purse or one of the children urgently required a new pair of shoes.

Some families had a crisis over money every week. Altogether six mothers borrowed money (anything between £1 and £3) from their neighbour every Wednesday or Thursday and paid it back on payday. Four more borrowed from relatives in the same way. Only three families mentioned that they used money-lenders. Other families resorted to the pawnshop or tried to find something they could sell. For example, Mrs. Foster, whose husband had become disabled and had had to give up his job as a bus driver, only received a training allowance of £10 while he was on a retraining course. This was supplemented by National Assistance and family allowances, bringing their total income to £17 14s. They had eight children, all under fifteen, so money was very short. During the twelve months prior to the interview she had sold her transistor radio and her sewing machine to buy food, and at the time of the interview was searching round the house for rags to sell. Two mothers had pawned their wedding rings—for fifteen shillings. When the money needed was a larger sum then sometimes the mother would go out to work in order to raise money. Four mothers reported going out cleaning to pay off rent arrears, for example.

Altogether only a quarter of the families had any kind of cash reserves of their own and half of these were in the top income group. Those families without any savings had to raise money in an emergency some other way and, as table 4.7 shows, over a third of the families were in debt at the time of the survey.[14]

TABLE 4.7

Number and Percentage of Families with Different Incomes who had Savings and Debts

Whether having Savings or Debts	Household Income as a per cent of National Assistance Scale							
	under 100		100 but less than 140		140 and over		All families[1]	
	N	%	N	%	N	%	N	%
Having savings	–	–	7	(22)	15	(48)	22	28
Having debts	15	(81)	10	(33)	5	(16)	30	38
Total	18	(100)	31	(100)	31	(100)	80	100

(1) All families excludes six whose income was unknown.

The poorest families were the least able to insure against the father's sudden illness or accident or even death. Altogether 80 per cent of the families had insurance policies of some kind, but among families with incomes under £20, only half had managed to keep up the payments on their policies, which were often only worth £50–£100. A family who fell behind with payments could have the policy cancelled without getting back anything for the years of weekly contributions. Child endowment policies, whereby for six-pence or a shilling a week, each child received between £15 and £50 when he leaves school were quite popular. Twenty-five families had taken out such policies so that each child would have something with which to buy new clothes and shoes when he or she started work.

The Problems of Housekeeping

The mother of any large family must be a 'good manager' but if at the same time the father's earnings are low, then she must be able to withstand considerable physical and mental strain. To be a 'good manager' on a small income requires an inexhaustible supply of self-discipline. She must limit herself to buying only as much as she can afford and no more, even though she knows this is not the cheapest way of buying. If she does spend too much on one thing then she must cut down elsewhere. This can mean watching every penny: 'I know that if I spent 1s 10d on cheese then 4d must come off something else because I've worked out that 1s 6d is as much as I ought to pay for it.' She may have to sit down every day to scheme

14. The Supplementary Benefit Commission's study of fifty-two wage-stopped families found half had been in rent arrears and two in every five had other debts. Supplementary Benefit Commission, *op. cit.*, p. 4.

out ways of making, for example, 22s pay for the daily needs of a family of eight. She must make sure the rent is paid, even if, as one mother did, she has to hand it to the next door neighbour to keep until rent week. Also she has to resist buying little treats for the children or for herself. In many ways this was one of the hardest things to do. Mr. Henshaw realized this when he handed over all the money to his wife to manage when he became dependent on National Assistance because of his ill health. 'I'd go out shopping and if I saw a little toy, or the children asked me for sweets, then I wouldn't be able to say no if I had the money in my pocket.' On the other hand, Mrs. Clegg complained when her husband would not give her extra housekeeping when he had earned a lot of overtime. However, he could not understand why because he always bought something special for tea those Fridays or bought extras for the children. He never spent it on himself. What he did not realize was that he was denying his wife the pleasure of 'splashing out' once in a while and buying things that were not strictly necessary. As Mrs. Langley said: 'It's like one big cycle—you get caught up in it and go on somehow from one week to the next hoping you'll get out of it. But you don't.'

5. HOUSEHOLD AND FAMILY ORGANIZATION

In this chapter we explore the overall household management of large families: the organization of housework and leisure both in normal circumstances and in emergencies; and also the kinds of restrictions the management of the household placed on the family's relationships and activities.

Much has been written about the changes in family relationships and in the status and role of women brought about by the demographic changes that have occurred since the beginning of this century, and particularly the decline in family size. It is generally concluded that childbearing and rearing has been reduced to an episode in the life of a married woman and that they have achieved partial emancipation from the domesticity that had been their lot for so long. This has brought about changes in the nature of marital relationships. Rosser and Harris, in their study of family life in Swansea, concluded: 'The greater the level of female domesticity, the stronger the cohesion of the extended family and the more effective its function of support for the individuals or elementary families who 'belong'. The decline in family size, the liberation of women from the rack of prolonged child bearing, the increased life expectancies (particularly for women), better educational and employment opportunities, more convenient hours and more household gadgets, better incomes, shorter working hours for men, holidays with pay, the great transformation in the relationships between husbands and their wives—all these factors at least have conspired to produce a profound social revolution in the status and attitudes and interests of women. So far as the effectiveness of the extended family is concerned, it is a change which is only just, 'with the daughters of revolution' beginning to exert its effects. This change in the position of women has been more sudden and more recent in working-class families than in the middle classes. There is a relationship between the degree of domesticity of women, the nature of the marital relationship and the shape of the external kinship network.

In Bott's terms,[1] the trend of change is always from the compulsive domesticity of women and thus towards 'joint' marital relationships of the partnership or companionship type, and towards 'loose-knit' external familial networks.'[2]

This is true for many women who have only one, two or three children but is it true for the mother of the large family? Is it no longer true that the addition of a child to a large family still means, as it did fifty years ago 'more crowding, more illness, more worry, more work and less food, less strength, less time to manage with'[3] or has increasing affluence removed or at least modified these hardships? This study did not set out to examine in detail the internal relationships of the large family for this would be a major study in itself. However, information was collected about the ways in which the management of the household was shared between each parent and between parents and children. While it is not possible to say that because the basic marital relationship was 'shared' or 'separated' they organized the family one way rather than another, the nature of the relationship came out in what each parent did. It also shows some of the ways in which the mother of the large family, except in the high income groups, has yet to be liberated from compulsory domesticity.

Housekeeping Responsibilities

The way in which family responsibilities were shared was reflected in the way in which the housekeeping money was managed. In general, the primary responsibility for managing the household finances shifted from the father in the higher income families to the mother in the low income families (see Table 5.1).

There were two reasons for this shift in responsibility. First, in all the families the mother paid for items bought frequently, and the fathers made the long-term payments: the majority of household payments were in the former category in the poorer families so inevitably the mother took over the purse strings.

Over half (fifty) of the mothers paid all the household expenses: rent, food, clothing, fuel, hire purchase payments, insurance and pocket money. However, among the working mothers over three-quarters (fifteen) paid all expenses, compared with half of those who did no paid work. Similarly, when the family could not rely on the father's earnings and became either substantially dependent on the mother's earnings, or completely dependent on State benefits, the

---

1. Bott describes a 'joint' relationship as one in which husband and wife share much of the work and decisions inside the home and have many interests in common outside. At the other extreme was the 'segregated' relationship which was based on a sharp division of labour and interests both inside and outside the home. For a further discussion see Bott, E. *"Family and Social Network"*, Tavistock Publications, London 1957, Chapter 3.
2. Rosser C. and Harris C. *"The Family and Social Change"*, Routledge and Kegan Paul, London 1965, p. 290.
3. Pember Reeves, M., *"Round About a Pound a Week"*. G. Bell & Sons, Ltd., London 1913, p. 153.

responsibility for managing the household affairs rested completely with the mother. As a result, all the mother's except two in the families with weekly incomes below the basic National Assistance level managed all the household affairs compared with only a third in the highest income group.[4]

TABLE 5.1

Number and Percentage of Families with Different Income According to Responsibility of Mother or Father for Household Expenditure

Responsibility for Household Expenditure	Household Income as per cent of National Assistance Scale						All families[1]	
	under 100		100 and under 140		140 and over			
	N	%	N	%	N	%	N	%
Father and mother jointly	2	(11)	11	(35)	20	(64)	36	44
Mother with								
(a) part of father's earnings	5	(28)	14	(44)	6	(19)	28	32
(b) all of father's earnings	11	(61)	6	(19)	5	(16)	22	24
Total	18	(100)	31	(100)	31	(100)	86	100

1) All families includes six for whom income data was unknown.

Secondly, families with low incomes depended less on the father's earnings. Apart from family allowances, many (thirty-six) had other sources of incomes besides the father's earnings, and fourteen were dependent on state benefits. The lower the father's basic wage the more likely was the household income to be supplemented in other ways.[5] If the father's earnings were unreliable, a second source of income at least guaranteed the mother a certain amount of house-keeping money. Mrs. Shawcross for example, who had a full-time job as a bottle washer, had more reliable earnings than Mr. Shaw-cross, a building labourer, who was epileptic and so could not always work a full week. Sometimes she even earned more than he did in a week. The money earned by the mothers was invariably used for the housekeeping.

Other sources of housekeeping apart from the father's earnings were very important. Altogether two-fifths (thirty-four) of the mothers relied on sources of income other than the father's earnings for the money with which to run the household. Most (fifteen) of the (eighteen) poorest mothers relied on other sources, but in the highest income group only a fifth did so. The money from these sources came direct to her and so were under her control alone.[6] Although

---

4. The National Assistance Board's policy of assessing entitlement on the father's claim, and paying benefit to him except in grave cases of mis-spending did not lead to budgeting difficulties among any of the large families interviewed.
5. See Chapter 2, p. 20.
6. Similar conclusions were drawn from a study of working wives in Bermondsey, 'Even if the wife's wages are small, they represent a measure of insurance and, furthermore, the money is under her own control'. Jephcott, P., Seear, N., and Smith, '*Married Women Working*', Allen and Unwin, Ltd., 1962, p. 102.

E

she always spent this money as part of the housekeeping, this money nevertheless decreased her economic dependence on her husband.[7] In effect, the father's role as breadwinner of the family was reduced in these families, the more so because the money the mother received from elsewhere was not 'pin-money' but vital to the household's economy. It was therefore very unlikely that the father of the poor, large family could retain complete economic control over the family. Their situation made some sharing in financial decisions inevitable.

Although a large proportion of mothers were responsible for the household payments, as the figures in Table 5.1 show, only a quarter of them were given all the father's earnings. In the poorest group a higher proportion (61 per cent) were given all earnings. Arrangements differed between the families. Sometimes the father handed over his entire wage packet, getting back travelling money and cigarette money. In other families the mother was given the wage packet less the overtime earnings or tips and only gave the father 'pocket money' if overtime or tips were very low that week. Among the salary earners the families either had a joint bank account or money was paid into the mother's account monthly for her to draw on as she needed. A minority of mothers (nineteen) were given fixed amounts of housekeeping and expected to manage without asking for more even if the father had earned extra overtime that week, and only nine of them were expected to pay for everything out of this fixed amount. Few (six) mothers did not know what their husbands earned although they had some idea. Only one mother complained about the amount of housekeeping money she was given: 'If I were a lady M.P. I'd introduce a standard rate of housekeeping based on a husband's money and the number of children.' However, this family was an exception.[8] 'We pool together,' was a frequently made remark, meaning the father's earnings were entirely at the disposal of the household even if he did not actually hand them over to the mother. Most families realized that in order to keep going a high degree of co-operation on money matters was essential.

Mothers' Work

We have shown in Chapter 2 that nineteen mothers were in paid employment. Eight of these mothers worked full time, and their earnings accounted for more than a fifth of the household income. Fitting in a paid job posed major organizational problems in running

---

7 The mothers of large families are no different in this respect from other working wives. 'The wife who worked appeared to derive her chief financial return for working by having money of her own, and her ability to spend more freely on her daily shopping, on food, and on the smaller articles of clothing and household goods.' Jephcott, Seear and Smith, *op. cit.*, p. 120–121.

8. The families drawn in the sample who were not willing to be interviewed may have contained a higher proportion of those in which the father was more secretive about his earnings.

a large household. However, although the economic reasons for a mother with several children going out to work were more pressing than for a mother with one or two children, she still required either working hours to enable her to be home when the children were, or a responsible adult known to the children with whom to leave them.

Only two mothers were able to rely on their mothers to look after the children while they worked during the day. In one instance the mother actually lived with the family and acted as housekeeper and baby minder; and in the other she lived near enough for the youngest children to be left with her during the day and for the school children to have a midday meal there. This latter arrangement, however, was not entirely satisfactory for both the eldest girls frequently played truant from school and with no one at home all day it was some time before their parents discovered their truancy and difficult for them to ensure they went and stayed at school. A further two mothers were paid for work they did in their own homes. In both cases they were sewing jobs for which they were paid on a piece-work basis. One mother was able to take a full-time secretarial job because all the children had started school and the older children were able to manage after school until she returned home. The other mothers had to arrange their working hours so that they were away from home at a time when a responsible adult could be in charge of the younger children. Usually this was the father, who after coming home from work had to give the children their supper and put them to bed. The majority of fathers appeared to enjoy this and welcome the chance to be with the children. However, after a long and tiring day's work some men found this too much to cope with and more than one evening interview was refused by a harassed father who was obviously fighting a losing battle with the bedlam that could be heard as soon as the front door opened. Mr. Southern complained that his wife's night-shift work meant not that he saw too much of the children, but that he did not see enough of her! Mrs. Sawyer and her husband both did shift work and arranged their work so that if one was working the night shift the other worked during the day.

Although these mothers had taken paid employment because the family needed the money, there was the compensation that it took them away from the house and often provided companionship. Mrs. Conway, the mother of nine, was glad of an excuse to get an evening job when her husband had to take a lower paid job. 'Sometimes I'd sit here cooped up with them all feeling I'd go mad if I didn't get out. My husband didn't like me going out to work but he had to admit we needed the money. I work on an assembly line in a factory, it was a bit difficult to start with—I was so nervous but now I've got to know some of the girls, they're ever so nice, even some of the coloured ones. As for leaving him to cope with the children, well he's got Joan to help him and it does him good.' Several mothers talked about the job they hoped to get once the children were old enough, not only in terms of the much needed money but in terms of the opportunity it would give them to have a break from the endless domestic chores. On the other hand, some of the other mothers while not grumbling directly commented: 'I hope my daughter never has to go out cleaning.'

Housework

Each mother had her own way of organizing the housework, and the more money she had the more freedom it gave her to plan her time as she wanted. The previous chapter has discussed the economies of scale the richer families could afford. This chapter shows how much of the drudgery from the housework money can remove.

The mothers who had generous housekeeping allowances were able to order the weekly groceries by telephone and have them delivered, or if the family preferred the supermarket the father or mother could take the car and collect the week's provisions. In both cases, the amount of fetching and carrying was reduced to a minimum. By contrast the poorer mothers bought their food daily, and as the last chapter showed, even bread and milk deliveries were stopped when money became very scarce. The poorer family's diet was more likely to contain bulky items and the tens of pounds of potatoes eaten every week by many of the poorer families not only had to be prepared but carried home. Similarly, the families who could afford to buy fuel in bulk not only benefited from the financial saving involved but had no cartage problems. Those who bought coal or paraffin several times a week did not necessarily have it delivered to the doorstep, especially if the family lived in a block of flats without lifts, and, as many of them were, several floors up. Buying little and often is an expensive method of buying in terms not only of money but of physical energy, both of which are very precious to the mother of a large family.

The poorer families did not possess labour-saving devices[9] such as a washing machine. Two mothers who had no machine of their own were able to use their neighbour's but most took the family's washing to the launderette. Here again this involved more fetching and carrying than if they had been able to do their washing in their own homes. Half (fifteen) of those without a washing machine went to the launderette at least three times a week. Mrs. Godfrey, however, was reluctant to use the launderette because she had four enuretic children and was ashamed to wash their dirty sheets in public. Besides, some of their sheets were only large pieces of rag because

9. See Chapter 4, Table 4.4, p. 54.

she could not afford to replace sheets which quickly rotted with such abnormal use. Instead she had to wash them by hand in the sink at home. Enuretic children cause extra difficulties and work in any family but where there is little money these difficulties are considerably increased.

Some mothers not only did the shopping, cooking, cleaning and washing but also had time to make clothes for themselves or the children. Altogether, a third (twenty-nine) of the mothers did some sewing or knitting. Among them was a mother who had eight children *and* a full-time job. As in all the other household jobs, the richer mothers were at an advantage partly because they had more time and partly because they could afford a sewing machine. The fact that two-thirds of the mothers who did their own sewing belonged to families in the top third of the income range was a reflection of this rather than any lack of skill among the poorer mothers. Two of the mothers in the lowest income group had had to sell their sewing machines. 'It was my pride and joy—a lovely little electric machine. I have to pay more for clothes now I know, but I couldn't keep it—we needed food,' explained Mrs. Foster whose husband had developed chronic heart trouble and for two years had been unable to work. Economizing and saving were luxuries she could no longer afford.

The richer families had the further advantage that their homes and particularly their kitchens were well designed and easy to run compared with the old, badly equipped houses and flats many of the family had to live in. Lack of adequate storage space introduced problems, each minor on its own but altogether made the mother's task of running the home much more difficult than it might have been. Mrs. Fuller explained the problem clearly: 'I have fifteen shirts to iron every week but there's nowhere to hang them so they get crumpled and need ironing again before they can wear them.' Piles of clean clothing could be seen lying around several living rooms we visited, 'the latest in sideboard decoration' as one mother described them.

Badly designed or cramped homes lacking storage space made it more difficult to keep anything tidy or remove breakable objects from the reach of young children, so the risk of breakages increased. The Salter family, for example, had gone through three complete dinner services in a year.

The mother's reactions to having to carry the burden of housework varied greatly. Some were quite unperturbed by this: 'People ask me how I manage with this crowd. All I say is that it's as easy to cook for nine as it is for two. I love cooking—I bake all our own bread and at weekends I make cakes and buns—it's much cheaper than buying them and you know they're made of fresh things.'

Altogether, eight mothers baked their own bread. Other mothers, however, found the work irksome: 'It seems all work—I have to do three big washes a week, so I'm up early most mornings. But there's so much else I never get to bed before one o'clock in the morning. It's the drudgery of it all—like peeling ten pounds of potatoes every day. Oh, I'm pleased if they all say they've enjoyed a meal I've cooked them, but I don't really get any pleasure out of cooking. I don't think I was cut out to be a mother,' said Mrs. Wright wearily. She had six children, the eldest aged ten, the youngest six months.

Money was the overriding factor which determined the extent of the burden of housework. The mothers who had sufficient money were able to buy labour saving devices which removed the drudgery associated with running a large household. The amount of housework they had to do was little more than for a two or three child family. Similarly, if most of the food a family needed could be delivered then the physical work involved in shopping was not greater than that for a smaller family. The poorer mothers were not only unable to buy in the most economical manner but also unable to conserve their energy. Each additional child in these families increased the mother's burden. The mothers could not afford to be inefficient in running the home, if they had been the family would have broken up. One of the richest mothers (the family's annual income was over £7,000) had every labour saving device, including a dishwashing machine, was right in a sense when she said, 'I am surprised you haven't asked more questions about domestic help—after all it is physically impossible to bring up six children single-handed.'

Sharing the Housework

While it was true that the larger the family the more the children helped, the majority of the children (60 per cent) were not expected to help regularly, although only 27 per cent gave no help at all.

Mothers with paid employment tried very hard not to off-load housework on to the children, and the proportion (35 per cent) of children helping these mothers regularly was not significantly different from the proportion (42 per cent) among families in which the mother had no paid employment. This was partly because they felt that childhood was a time for play. They also felt that although economic necessity took them out to work, it was wrong that the children should be further penalized by giving them chores to do.

However, where mothers did early morning cleaning jobs they could not always be back in time to get the family's breakfast. One mother relied on her eldest son to get the children their breakfast. At the time of the survey she was looking for a job nearer home so that she could be back earlier. Mothers with paid employment could have pushed the burden of running the home on to their elder children, but the majority did not do so and one of the main reasons given by the mothers in this study for not going out to work was that they knew no *adult* with whom to leave the children.

The ways in which the children helped varied between the richer and poorer families. Children's help was less important to the mother who had mechanical aids. The help given by them was seen more as an aspect of character training. For example, the teenage children of a surveyor's family were expected to make their own beds, help with washing-up at weekends and keep their own rooms reasonably tidy. Their mother explained that she limited the amount of help asked of them, especially during school term time because they had homework to do and this had to come first. However, she believed strongly that they should learn to give her some assistance because it was good training and they should not grow up expecting every-thing to be done for them. The children of the large families in the higher income groups were not involved in the running of the household because the mother needed extra pairs of hands. Their involvement in household chores was probably little different from that of their friends from smaller families.

The household duties of the teenage children of some of the lower income families were very different and often much more strenuous. After coming home from school they were expected to go shopping, fetch paraffin or coal, take a load of washing to the launderette; or if the mother felt they could not manage this, they looked after the younger children while she went herself. These were the children who were likely to have been up early in the morning helping to deliver newspapers or milk. The children of these families shared the physical strain involved in bringing up a large family on a low income and it was the reluctance of the majority of the mothers to involve them in just this that made them ask their children for help only occasionally. As Mrs. Timms said, 'I believe children should be allowed to be children and just play: they shouldn't have to spend all their time doing odd things for me. They'll learn life is hard soon enough, let them enjoy it while they can.'[10] On the other hand, her husband held just the opposite view, believing that helping in the home was good character training: 'It's ridiculous, she goes

10. Placing more importance on present pleasure than on events in the future is more common among working class than middle-class families and reveals a same difference in attitude towards the future. As Bernstein concludes from his studies of the linguistic development of children among middle class and working class families, the latter's environment 'limits the perception of the developing child of and in time. Present gratification or present deprivation become absolute gratification or absolute deprivation, for there exists no developed time – continuous upon which present activity can be ranged relative to the middle-classes, the postponement of present pleasure for future gratification is found difficult'. Bernstein B., Social Class and Linguistic Development. A theory of social learning. *Education, Economy and Society* edited by A. H. Halsey, Jean Floud and C. Arnold Anderson. Collier Macmillan Ltd., London 1961, p. 297. This is also discussed further in this report on p. 88 and pp. 137.

out cleaning every evening and when she comes home has to do all the washing and clearing up. If only she'd get the children to help a bit she wouldn't have all that to do when she gets back feeling tired. It was different when I was young. I was brought up in a mining village and life was tough then. When I was only seven I had to get up first every morning to fetch coal and light the fire. They have it too easy these days.' The difference in attitude of the mother and father towards helping in the home runs through many working class attitudes, in particular to education. There was however, no difference between the amount of help given by boys and girls. The boys helped in the home just as much as the girls.

There was not a high (reported) incidence of children being kept from school because their help was needed at home. Altogether only fifteen of the schoolchildren (8 per cent) who had missed any school in the past two terms had been absent for that reason. Truancy accounted for just as many absences, but the main reason (79 per cent) for a child's absence from school was his or her own illness. The mother who always kept her fourteen year old son home if she was ill or if the baby was ill and she could not go out shopping was an exception.[11]

Help in Emergencies

The mother was the key figure in the running of the large family household. What happened in an emergency: when she was ill or when she was having a baby? Who looked after the children and did the housework? The way in which the families solved these problems depended on two things: the availability of outside help from relatives, friends or neighbours, and their willingness to call upon this help.

In emergencies the father was the most likely member of the family to stay at home and help—often sacrificing earnings or holiday entitlement—or both. Two fathers had lost their jobs because they had been needed at home for a prolonged period. Fifty-three of the families (61 per cent) had been looked after by the father either on his own or with the help of the eldest son or daughter at the birth of the last baby. In sixteen families the eldest child had managed the whole family unassisted. Only five fathers had been helped by a relative other than his own children and only one had been helped by a neighbour. Altogether five families had had a home help (none with a weekly income below £20) although one other family had been offered one and refused partly because they could not see how a home help working part-time could possibly look after nine children. The younger children in two families had been taken into care. Only ten families had been able to rely on the help

---

11. Absence from school is discussed more fully in Chapter 6, p. 90 and p. 91.

of a grandmother or aunt, which was an indication of the limited role relatives played in the lives of many of these large families.[12]

There was however a strong reluctance among some mothers to leave their children to manage without them. Several mothers expressed the feeling that they owed it to their children to stay with them and that however many material things the children went short of, they were not going to be deprived of their mother. As one mother said, 'All they've got is us.' This was why they refused to let their children be taken into care in a crisis, and why even if they had been offered a home help would not have entrusted their children to the care of a stranger. Mrs. Green had recently discharged herself from hospital where she had been under observation for six weeks because she was suspected of having T.B. and was six months pregnant. She felt unable to stay away from home, even though she knew she ought to be in hospital. 'It's the worry you know—men aren't like us, they don't understand how we feel about leaving children. When I had the last baby I had a real bad time of it—I was away a month and the children were shocked with me being away so long. It's their little nerves you know, David still wakes up screeching for me and he sometimes wets the bed, though he'd stopped when he was five. It's not right to leave them—you have to watch their little minds. And I wouldn't give my children anywhere—there's no one like your own mother.'

A quarter (twenty-one) of the mothers said they often felt ill, ill enough to want to stay in bed. However, only seven of them had been able to stay in bed when feeling like this during the last month. 'I feel all run down at times, all nervified. But I can't afford to be ill so I just grin and bear it,' said Mrs. John who had seven children.

Another reason for refusing to admit to being ill was the desire to continue working. Mrs. Fulcher, whose eldest daughter wanted to stay on in the sixth form was determined to go on with her job in spite of having a bad heart and in spite of repeated warnings from her doctor to give up her work. Yet another reason for a mother not taking things easy when she felt unwell was that the family lived in such cramped conditions that there was nowhere in the house where she could get any peace and quiet. There was little point in going to bed.

Altogether, nearly half (forty) mothers said it was very difficult to make arrangements for the children to be looked after and the housework done if they were unable to do it themselves. This suggests (if these large families are representative) that the poorer large family is often physically isolated from relatives and feels socially isolated from neighbours. This isolation is reinforced by lack of money.

---

12. Contact with and availability of help from relatives is discussed on pp. 74–77.

Hence they see themselves or are forced to see themselves as a self-sufficient unit seeking help from each other but not from 'outsiders'.

Help from Relatives

One important reason for the small part played by relatives in the lives of the large families was that surprisingly few of them were part of a close, extended family network. In the first place, over half (fifty-three) the families had no living grandparents on one or both sides and only fifteen families had all four grandparents living. In the second place, many of the parents of the large families had moved both before marriage (looking for employment) and after marriage (looking for accommodation). This inevitably meant some had become physically separated from their own parents and siblings. Seventeen couples had no siblings at all living within half an hour's journey from them and twelve couples had no parents living nearby. Only nineteen mothers and nineteen fathers were still living in the borough in which they were born compared with twenty-nine families in which both parents had been born outside of London. Altogether the parents of twenty-five families had been born and brought up outside of England, most (eighteen) of them in Ireland. Therefore, only a little over a third (thirty) of the mothers and twenty-seven of the fathers had one or both parents living within half an hour's journey from them. Rather more (fifty-two fathers, fifty-three mothers) had at least one sibling living within that distance. However, even if parents and siblings were living nearby, they were not necessarily seen frequently. Only fifteen fathers and twenty-one mothers saw their own mothers at least once a week.[13] A third of mothers and fathers saw their siblings once a week.[14] As many had had no contact for over a year.

Daily contact with grandparents was rare and occurred only when they were actually living in the same house or living 'round the corner'. Altogether, the grandparents of eighteen families were part of their daily life. Four families lived with grandmother, three having moved in because it was the only accommodation they could find.

When grandparents lived very close, the whole family usually saw a great deal of them. Mrs. Godfrey's mother, for example, had two

---

13. This is a significantly lower proportion at the one per cent level, than Wilmott and Young found in their study of families in Woodford. There 63 per cent of married people whose mothers were still living saw them at least once a week, compared with 40 per cent (36) of the parents of the large families in this study. Wilmott, P. and Young, M., *Family and Social Class in a London Suburb*, Routledge, Kegan and Paul, London 1960, p. 66.

14. These are significantly lower proportions (at the one per cent level) than Rosser and Harris found among the families interviewed in Swansea. There half the men and two-thirds of the women had seen a brother or sister living apart in the same week. Frequency of contact depended not only on the proximity of relatives but also whether the subject's parents were alive, particularly the mother, because the parental home was a family meeting place. Rosser C. and Harris C., *op. cit.*, p. 222.
    Twenty-seven of the families in this study either had no grandmother living or they were not living nearby.

of the children stay with her every weekend, 'Well, it's no trouble for me and they enjoy it. Since my old man died last year I've been on my own and four walls aren't much company.' She had found a part-time job at a transport cafe nearby and during the week called in on the family on her way home for a cup of tea and a chat. Only one other family had this arrangement. Mr. Sawyer called on his mother every day on his way home from work and she always gave him a pint of milk for the family. Grandparents in these circumstances often gave the children pocket money or other little treats. Even Mr. Talbot's father still visited the children to bring them sweets and fresh fruit (he had a fruit barrow in the local market) although his son had left Mrs. Talbot and her eight children eighteen months ago.

Daily contact with siblings was rarer, only eight mothers and six fathers saw at least one sibling every day. They lived in the same house or very close by. In order to maintain a mutually helpful relationship with relatives it seemed essential for the large family to live only a short distance away. Lack of time and money inhibited the maintenance of a close relationship over longer distances. For example, Mrs. Ogden used to visit her mother two or three times a week, but when the 'bus fare went up to a shilling she found it cost too much, especially as she usually had to take two of the children with her. The cost of transporting six or seven children even for short distances was prohibitive for many families and it was not always possible for the other members of the family to visit them. Mrs. Conway used to have a telephone until Mr. Conway became redundant and was unemployed for six months. 'My eldest boy has promised to have one installed again because we miss it so much. Whenever I'm in trouble I turn to my brother but he lives in Birmingham. It was lovely when I could just 'phone him and he could 'phone me regularly. The nearest public telephone that works is fifteen minutes away so I only 'phone him if I'm really desperate—it's not the same.' As Table 4.4 shows, only one in five families had their own telephones and nearly half of these were in the highest income group. A telephone was way beyond the means and expectations of most families.

In their study of family life in Swansea Rosser and Harris found that although many families no longer lived in the close-knit communities of fifty years ago, they were nevertheless able to maintain a high degree of contact between relatives especially between parents and grown-up children. They noted that 'if the dispersal of the extended family within Swansea has had little effect on frequencies of visiting, at any rate between parents and unmarried children, this is due to good internal communications and increase in car ownership' and conclude 'there seems good reason to regard communications as social services which can play an important role in maintaining the extended family in its dispersed form.'[15] The results of this study would seem to indicate that unless a large family has a high income they are unable to take advantage of improvements in communications (see Table 4.4) but at the same time they are forced to move away from the locality in which they were brought up in order to find work or accommodation. Inevitably they are unable to maintain relationships with relatives, and in particular are unable to look to their support in times of trouble.[16]

However, it may also be that in addition to the difficulty of overcoming *physical* distance from relatives, some of the factors that contributed to isolation from neighbours may also help to explain the large families' isolation from relatives, particularly siblings. Although half of the parents of the families in this study themselves came from large families, at the time of the survey the majority of their siblings had had less than five children. Only eight of the fathers and thirteen of the mothers who came from large families had one or more siblings with at least five children, and half of these parents were in the highest income group.[17] Altogether among all the families in this study, fourteen fathers and twenty-one mothers (this included nine couples) had siblings with large families. The majority of couples in this study were therefore different from their siblings who had had small families. It is therefore possible that the elements of hostility found in neighbours' and workmates' attitudes towards the poorer large families were shared by some of their siblings.[18] For example Mrs. Sawyer said of her sisters who lived outside London, 'Oh, I know they come up to see my mother quite often, but they never bother to come here. It wouldn't be much trouble but they think we're not grand enough. They don't want to know you if you've got lots of children.' Another mother said she was often teased about her large family: 'You're just like your mother!' In addition, some of the large families themselves were likely to feel poor compared with their siblings, they were therefore reluctant to ask for help in the same way that some of them tried to

15. Rosser, C. and Harris, C., *op. cit.*, pp. 299–300.
    Wilmott and Young also found in their study of families in Woodford that distance affected contacts with relatives less among middle-class families than among working class families. They suggested that the reason for this was the fact that middle-class families were more likely to own a car and telephone. Moreover these families had room for relatives to stay and time to write more often. Wilmott, P. and Young, M., *op. cit.*, p. 79 seq.
16. Rosser and Harris suggest that in times of crises such as child bearing and illness, a family needs more than purely material services. The importance of help from relatives on such occasions lies "in its ability to provide support for its members at times of difficulty and this support is effective because of the strong emotional ties between members . . . The provision of this type of care, which might be described as 'affective' is likely to continue to be of importance whatever changes may occur in the domestication of women". Rosser C. and Harris C., *op. cit.*, p. 297.
    The experiences of the large families in this study suggest that they seek 'affective' care from each other rather than from relatives living apart from the family.
17. This is not because they were all the eldest in the family. Twenty of the mothers and nine of the fathers from large families were first or second children but sixteen of the mothers and twenty-three of the fathers were a fifth or younger child from a large family.
18. Unfortunately questions about the attitudes of the parents' siblings towards them and their large families were not asked systematically. The above conclusions can only be very tentative therefore.

avoid asking the help of neighbours because of their inability to reciprocate.[19]

Regular Relief from Housework

'It's Mum this and Mum that all day long. I feel choked by demands. Sometimes I could throttle them—but that feeling only lasts a second, mind,' said Mrs. Walters, expressing a feeling several mothers had from time to time. As the previous section has shown it was not easy for many of the mothers to delegate their household responsibilities completely for any length of time. But how many were able to escape just once in a while from the demands of the family?

Altogether thirty-two mothers had at least one evening out in the two weeks preceding the interview—half of them with their husbands. They would visit relatives, spend an evening in the pub or perhaps go to bingo. However, seventeen of the mothers who had never had a holiday away also never went out in the evenings, unless it was to work.

There were various reasons for not going out, not all of them financial. Some parents did not want to go out, 'I know you'll think we're foolish—I'm sure lots of our friends do, but you know, we enjoy just sitting here together by the fire when the children are in bed. I don't want to go out and about, I like my own home,' explained Mrs. Queen who had six children and very obviously enjoyed having a large family. Others would not go out because they would not entrust their children to a babysitter, even if it was a relative. Mr. and Mrs. Webster would have liked to go out some evenings but they never did so, even though her mother lives opposite. 'Well, I know she would babysit but she's getting an old lady now and the children might play her up. Of course, David the eldest boy says he could manage now he's twelve and I expect he could. But you never know—supposing something happened while we were out, I'd never forgive myself,' explained Mrs. Webster. Some, however, did wish they had occasional evenings out—even if it was just a meal cooked by someone else. Others would have gone out if they had had something smart to wear. It cost more money than some mothers could afford to take as much pride in their appearance as they would have liked. In just the same way they were reluctant to have visitors because they had no 'decent' front room.

Some mothers were quite happy to go out on their own and did not let their husbands' lack of enthusiasm or energy deter them. Mrs. Maxwell, who described her husband as 'a dead drone' who would not go out unless compelled to, nevertheless lead an active life outside the home. Twice a week she helped at an old people's

---

19. Relationships with neighbours are discussed in Chapter 6, pp. 81–84.

club and on Sunday went round entertaining 'old folk' with a group of teenagers. Mr. Maxwell was an active member of the Rotary Club, but apart from that seemed quite content to stay at home with the children.

The richer mothers did go out with the family regularly but they nevertheless felt tied to the home. They envied their friends with smaller families or no children who could go away for a weekend on the spur of the moment and had much more time to pursue a particular interest, such as music or the theatre. There was a limit to the amount of time even money could buy.

Holidays

There were different ideas of what constituted a holiday. Some found a week of day trips returning each night to familiar surroundings much less trouble than a holiday away in more spartan surroundings. For example, Mrs. Charter had had a holiday with her mother-in-law and the children in a bungalow on Romney Marsh a few years ago. One of the children fell off a sea wall and had to be taken to the doctor; it rained and was cold. One week was more trouble than if she had stayed at home. Other families, however, did not consider they had had a holiday unless it was spent away from home.[20]

Taking the whole family away for a holiday was a major operation because transport had to be arranged as accommodation, and sometimes until a family had adequate transport of their own, a holiday away was out of the question. All but one of the families who owned a car (or more often a minibus) had managed to have a holiday in the previous year. Mr. and Mrs. Clarke and their eleven children had their first holiday a year ago when Mr. Clarke had bought a minibus with the money he received by cashing his insurance policy. He felt that not only was it time they had a family holiday, but with their own transport they could afford to go for day trips. Public transport was expensive and such a large family always attracted attention so Mrs. Clarke was continually being upset by the comments made by other passengers.

Six of the families hired a caravan or large continental tent and went camping. Mrs. Talbot remembered the holidays she used to have before her husband left her. 'We used to go off in his lorry with three or four other families and go camping. There were about thirty of us sometimes, but it was great fun because we used to share all the work: we'd take turns cooking, washing-up and so on. The children always enjoyed themselves too—they don't see much of the country now.' However, even camping could be beyond the

---

20. Because of these different views, families were asked not whether they had been *away* for a holiday but simply whether they had had one.

means of many families: a fortnight's caravan holiday for Mr. and Mrs. Trent and the nine children had cost £100.

For the poorer families even a day trip cost too much. As Mrs. Jenkins explained, 'I took four of them to Battersea Fun Fair because I'd promised them I would. I'll never do it again. It cost three and six to get in but then on top of that it cost seven bob for them all to go on just one thing. Then they all wanted an ice cream and I couldn't say no, after all it was their day out.' Others were reluctant to visit friends or relatives with the whole family, not so much because of the expense but because they felt it would not be fair. 'We can't descend on people with our crowd—it wouldn't be right.'

Only one mother had had a free holiday.[21] She had been very ill when the last baby was born and her doctor had arranged for her to spend three weeks by the sea. Mrs. Curtis had been offered a free holiday but had refused. 'They want to send me away convalescent, but I can't see the point in my going. I'd have to take the three younger children with me, so what sort of holiday would that be?' Over a third of the parents had never had a holiday since their marriage. As the previous section has shown, the father of the large family often spent his holiday looking after the children during the mother's illness. Other fathers never took their holiday entitlement or if they did found a second job to supplement their low holiday pay. Although a holiday was not part of their experience and they did not expect one, many nevertheless wanted or felt they needed one. As Mrs. Timpkins said, 'I ache all over, the doctor says I'm very run down. I'm taking some capsules. But you need a holiday don't you?'

Conclusions

The division of responsibility for managing and running the home varied considerably, although insufficient money placed certain restrictions on the poor families and insufficient time placed other restrictions on the richer families. At one extreme were the poorer families in which the mother not only had almost complete charge of the family's finance but made many of the decisions also. For example, Mrs. Wainwright said, 'He won't take any responsibility— I have to do everything, see to everything. When I told him about Johnny and the trouble he was in with this man (her twelve-year-old son was 'interfered' with by an older man) it was me who had to go to the police station, to go court and so on. All he said was 'Oh' when I told him. I'm sure if I told him I was flying to the moon all he'd say would be 'Oh'. At the other extreme were the parents who tried as much as possible to achieve a 'joint' relationship and financial decisions were not left to mother or father alone. This was

---

21. Free holidays for mothers are discussed further in Chapter 7, p. 104.

difficult, however, even for the high income families. Although they were much freer from time-consuming domestic chores, the children needed so much attention that there had to be a division of labour between mother and father: 'We never seem to have any time for ourselves. I tend to look after the younger ones while my husband spends his time with the older ones. It has to be like that, because we can't do everything as a family, the older ones feel the babies are holding them back. It's difficult always to find activities we can all do together,' said the bank manager's wife.

The mother of the large family had quite clearly not been freed from continual and prolonged domesticity. Therefore, by Rosser and Harris' hypothesis we would expect the relationship between husband and wife to be 'segregated' rather than 'joint'. On the other hand, neither the mother nor the father were involved in an external network of kin, or of friends. They looked for support either from each other or from their children. Their roles, therefore, were segregated in the sense that they were specialized, but based on co-operation as this was necessary in order to maintain the family as a group. Their roles also had to be interchangeable to a certain extent the mother sometimes acted as partial breadwinner by taking paid employment and the father sometimes took over the housekeeper's role during crises, which were frequent owing to regular pregnancies and a large number of children to look after. Also, the older children at times had to take over parental responsibilities either in full or in part.

The large family simply because of its size can only be organized and held together as a group if the mother and the father take on different but complementary roles. The mother of the poorer large families, like her own mother before her, was tied to a continual round of domestic chores because she could not afford labour-saving devices. The mother of the richer large families, although free of much of the drudgery, *unlike* their mothers and grandmothers could not rely on nannies and other domestic help to relieve them of the constant demands for time and attention made by their children. The place of the mother of the large family was still very much 'in the home'.

6. THE LARGE FAMILY AND THE COMMUNITY

A family with more than four children is exceptional and so attracts attention.[1] This chapter discusses both the informal and formal relationships the families had with the community in which they lived. These relationships are described as the family reported them, the descriptions are not, therefore, objective. Members of a low-paid wage-earner's large family felt that they were regarded with hostility. They were therefore more likely to interpret other people's behaviour toward them in an unfavourable way. Richer families did not encounter hostile attitudes.

Neighbours

Relationships with neighbours were often fraught with difficulties. Altogether ten families reported frequent incidents with neighbours, and six more talked about the difficult time they had had in their previous accommodation with neighbours. All but one of these families had a weekly income below £22.

Lack of money made it difficult for some families to take account of their neighbours as much as they would have liked, especially those living in blocks of flats. The poorer families covered their floors with linoleum : carpet was too expensive. When their children ran around the flat they inevitably disturbed the people living below.[2] It was impossible to keep the children quiet all the time. As Mrs. Walters said, 'You can't repress everything.' Similarly, lack of adequate play space outdoors gave less opportunity for children to work off their surplus energy where no one was inconvenienced. Children who could only play along the communal balconies and stairs annoyed the neighbours. Several mothers reported very strained and even hostile encounters with them.

---

1. Bossard made a similar comment in a study of large families in the United States. 'Size of family calls attention to itself per se, and this makes for an awareness of itself. There is the constant reminder of the family because of deprivations and limitations, as well as of the joys and satisfactions which it brings. There are the continuing comments of friends and neighbours. This apparently begins early in life for the children reared in large families. Their school mates tease them, the teachers refer to it and their friends joke about it.' Bossard, J. '*The Large Family System*' University of Pennsylvania Press 1956, p. 312. The situation of the large family in this country seemed to be similar.
2. See Chapter 3, p. 36.

Mrs. Green had not been happy in all the six years she had been in her present flat (which was on the fourth floor), 'It's terrible this district—I don't like the roughness. They said we'd only be here six months when we came here from Newington Lodge. Four years ago we signed a transfer form and then a year ago we were offered a flat but like this it wasn't on the ground floor. What's the point of taking a place where you'd be bound to get complaints from neighbours? I have enough trouble here—the woman along the balcony is always screeching at the little ones for playing on their little trike along the balcony. I put a gate across to stop them going too far but they learnt to get over it. She says I should take them down to the courtyard, but I can't keep an eye on them down there and I daren't leave the little ones alone. The other children are so rough: David's always getting into fights. Only last month he had to have stitches in the cuts he got while fighting. Then last week I went down there and there was this big boy nearly throttling him—turning blue he was—I got there in the nick of time. It's their mothers put them up to it—I've heard them tell them not to play with my children. Mind you, they're quite happy to take sweets or anything my children offer them—they're good and always share things even though they don't get so many. Two days ago all me washing was pinched—all their best little jumpers I had hanging out there to dry. I asked my man to bring them in last thing but he forgot. Oh, I've a good idea who took them—they don't like us around here. I wouldn't dare steal little woollies, I'd know if my children wore them they'd get run down crossing the road or something. Perhaps me luck will change when the little one is born— you can never tell with the little fairies. All I want is a little house and garden away from this place. Me luck must turn one day, don't you think.'

Mrs. Green blamed most of her difficulties on the neighbourhood in which she was living and she felt convinced that if only she and the family could move to a house and garden in a quieter area, all her problems would be solved. Although it was very easy for a mother in her situation to project the blame for all the family's problems on to the neighbours, Mrs. Green was quite clearly justified in believing she was living in a situation which inevitably created friction.

Two mothers had literally come to blows with neighbours. One did so because she could no longer stand the constant nagging from the woman in the flat above whenever her children so much as bounced a ball in the courtyard. She had been taken to court as a result but was conditionally discharged. Mrs. McClean had seen red when she heard her neighbour call after her little girl who was enuretic, 'Here comes stinky McClean. Go back to your own house and your stinky family.' She had stormed down the garden path and thrown a milk bottle at her, which luckily, as she admitted afterwards, had missed her and smashed to pieces on the door post.

The children were not always the cause of friction. Mrs. Walters was ostracized by all except one of her neighbours because they dscovered that her husband had appeared in court for indecently assaulting a little girl. Luckily she was befriended by one woman who even used to take her in the car to the supermarket once a week to fetch the groceries. Mrs. O'Shea used to get on very well with her next door neighbour until she had had a nervous breakdown and was sent home to Ireland for a holiday by her doctor. She took the baby with her and left her husband to look after the other six children with the assistance of a home help. 'Just as I was leaving she came out into the garden and called out such terrible things. She said what a wicked thing I was doing going off and leaving my children. What kind of mother did I think I was. When I came back she ignored me. We used to be such friends, she was always in and out. She was the sort of person that if you were feeling miserable she'd come in and put a kettle on and make a cup of tea and then you'd feel better. I could do with someone like her now. I often just sit and weep—I can't help it. This house is my prison.' Mrs. Clifford had a constant battle with her neighbours downstairs: 'You see, with my husband being epileptic he sometimes has a fit in the night and I have to run out and get help. Sometimes when I get back I find that the doors have been locked on me. They put the latch down so I can't get in. They're terrible with the children too. We're supposed to have access to the garden but they complain if any of them go near it. You'd think they'd understand— they've got two children of their own.'

For the majority of families, neighbours played no active part in their lives, although some had to put up with frequent comments about their large family. 'They don't expect you to have nothing if you've got children—they're catty people opposite. Just because we've got a front room they're always passing remarks. My husband's very handy, he did all this in the front room himself.' Other mothers described their neighbours as only 'good morning' types.

However, the little contact some families had with those living near them was not always a result of hostility or even indifference on the part of their neighbours. Isolation could arise from lack of money rather than from the exceptional size of their families. Several mothers felt a reluctance to ask for help when they felt they were not in a position to reciprocate. The closest relationships seemed to occur between families in similar situations. One mother said: 'We don't know anyone round here except the woman over the road and she's got ten children.' Another said: 'Oh, we're always borrowing from each other—we're in the same boat—always hard up.' Although some mothers knew their neighbours would help them more, they deliberately avoided asking them for as much help as they could have been given. As Mrs. Baldock explained: 'My neighbour next door has been like a second mother to me. She gave me a little chest of drawers when we first moved in—said she no longer needed it. She's given me shoes, too. Every Thursday she gives me two pounds of sugar and I pay her back early in the week. In return I cooked dinner for her and her old man while she was ill before Christmas. She insisted on giving me a present of some slippers in return. Still, I wasn't well last week but I didn't let on to her, I knew she'd offer to help and I didn't want that. She does enough for me.'

Altogether, less than one in four (seventeen) mothers had a mutually helpful relationship with neighbours. Rightly or wrongly, some families did not want to be continually receiving help, and chose to keep themselves to themselves. Others were not given the choice: their neighbours resented them and their children, and so added to their difficulties by unkind remarks and in some cases unkind actions. In addition, several of the poorer mothers had to put up with comments from the general public, although most took no notice. As Mrs. Caulder said: 'When I'm out with the kiddies, I'm always getting remarks like "What do you do in your spare time", or "You've been busy haven't you". So I say "Yes and there's more indoors and all". That shuts 'em up.'

The Fathers at Work

The fathers of a large family did not have so many dealings with neighbours, but several had to put up with continual comments from the men they worked with. Some of them felt this very keenly. For example, Mr. Southgate when asked about family allowances replied: 'I'd rather not have them at all for all the trouble they cause. They're always going on at me at work about how they're keeping my children—I don't pay any tax *and* I'm given family allowances, whereas half the money they earn is taken away in taxes so the Government can pay me the allowances. I get fed up with this moaning and groaning nearly every pay day. I can see how they feel. If they do a lot of overtime then most of it seems to go in taxes, whereas if I do overtime then I keep most of it. It causes a lot of bitterness, I don't think it's the right way to go about it. I don't mean I'm not grateful, but I didn't ask for the allowances and it is charity after all. It would be much better to tackle the cost of living, especially food prices—that would please everybody. I don't really know why they've kept family allowances—I've often wondered why.' He felt uncomfortable about receiving help when it was given in this form and would rather see food prices kept down because this would help other families as well as his own and he would not feel he had been singled out for special assistance.

Opportunity to do overtime could be a bone of contention between family men and single men. Some fathers felt that everyone should be given an equal opportunity to do it, while others believed the family man should be given priority. Then there were those who believed that because of the tax system it worked out in practice that only the man with children opted to do overtime anyway, because, as Mr. Southgate was constantly being reminded, it was not worth a single man's while to work overtime. Mr. Clarke, the father of eleven, had to put up with remarks of a more personal nature. 'It's not just the things they're always saying about family allowances and how they're keeping my children. They keep telling me I should do this or that not to have children. But I try to be a good Roman Catholic, so my conscience won't let me do any of these things they're always on about, unless the Church changes its view on birth control. Perhaps things will get better for Roman Catholics and perhaps large families will get a special dispensation to use the pill.'

On the other hand, Mr. Farthing did not let comments about his six children upset him. 'Oh, yes—I get teased, but it's like water off a duck's back. It's one of our fiercest arguments. I think family allowances are an investment for the country—think of the taxes and so on my children will be paying when they grow up. They'll be paying for the pensions of all those who go on at me now. As I say to my barber when he goes on about how dreadful it is that people still have a lot of children— "Look, you forget that when you only cut my hair you got three and sixpence. Now I take the two boys and you get ten shillings." That's what I mean about it being good for business.' One father explained that he was never teased because he worked with the Irish.

There was a grain of truth both in the attacks and in the justifications the fathers gave in return. The resentment the fathers of large families stirred up among their fellow workers was understandable and to some extent based on economic rivalry. When this was removed much of the resentment disappeared, for the attitude of those with whom the richer families worked was very different. They did not censure the fathers of large families. On the contrary, these men gained considerable kudos from having six or seven children. They were not made to feel irresponsible for having had more than the average number of children. Neither were they constantly reminded of the value of family allowances and—even more important for these families—of the value of allowances for children in the income tax.

A few (six) employers gave the father of the large family little extras. One man was given clothes for the family by his employer's wife. Another was allowed to use the firm's van at weekends provided he bought the petrol. A few provided interest free loans when the family was really hard up. Mr. Farthing was given the free cinema tickets his employer received for the local cinema in return for advertising their films in his shop. However, the steadier the father's job and the longer he had been with a particular firm the more likely he was to get special consideration. The poorer families by contrast, in which the father was likely to be frequently in and out of work for sickness or other reasons was unlikely to get assistance, although it was just these men who needed it most.

The Children at School[3]

The mothers of the poorer families were unable to provide all the extras for school that most other children had. As a result their children were involved in numerous incidents, scarcely significant in themselves but sufficient to cause the children concerned much hardship.

Many of these incidents centred round the mother's inability to clothe her children as well as other mothers. For example, children without a complete school uniform could be made to feel very awkward and were sometimes left out of school activities for that reason. Mrs. Charter's daughter, for example, was left off a school outing because she had no beret. Mrs. Finch felt so strongly about her son being picked on that she removed him from the school. 'One of the nuns stood him up in front of the whole class and told him off for not having a proper uniform. I'd sent him there for the religion and the education, not the uniform, so I took him away.' Another mother was having a prolonged battle with her son's new headmaster who had tightened up the rules concerning uniform. He wanted the boy to have a school scarf but his mother refused to spend thirty-five shillings on something her son had told her he would refuse to wear. He had the basic uniform and she always tried to send him looking clean and tidy and she thought that was sufficient. Sometimes it was other schoolchildren who made the child feel awkward. Three mothers reported children coming home from school in tears because of what prefects had said about their shoes or clothing.

There were other additional expenses which were beyond the purses of some families. They nevertheless tried to provide their

---

3. Information was collected by Mrs. Hilary Rose and Mrs. Ruth Michaels of the London School of Economics, from the teachers and head teachers of 75 per cent of the school children from these large families, during September 1966 and March 1967. This included 169 Primary and 106 Secondary School children. The author is indebted to them for allowing her to use some of their material in the following sections.

Readers are reminded that the sample is biased towards the *very* large family. (See Appendix I.).

children with them, so that they could join in all the activities with their classmates. For example, some mothers, while managing to buy the basic uniform, could not afford all the extra sports equipment, which could be very expensive. 'I know just how they feel—I was a scholarship child and I always felt left out of things. But what can I do? For instance, if they go swimming they've *got* to wear a special black costume which is twice as dear as an ordinary one,' explained one mother sadly. Altogether fifty-two (30 per cent) of the secondary school children had to provide extra money for sewing, cookery or woodwork classes. Sometimes this meant the child had to purchase materials, and sometimes it meant the parents had to supply them. Either way it could be expensive for, as Mrs. Compton explained, 'It's all right some of the time—it only comes to a bob or two. Last week, though, they made something fancy which cost over eight bob, and then when she brought it home there was only really enough for one. I can't afford to feed them at eight bob a head. But they want to be the same as the others in their class, so I have to give it them.'

Children in receipt of free school meals could be made to feel as awkward as those without a complete school uniform. As a result children asked their mothers to pay, 'Please pay, because if you're a free school meal child you're marked for life,' said one fourteen year old to her mother.[4]

The Children's Progress at School

All the mothers were asked how their children got on at school. Their answers gave little objective information on the child's academic progress. However they did reveal a little about the mothers' attitude towards her children's education and the extent of her contact with the schools they attend. When asked about one of the children's progress at school, several mothers answered at first in terms of how the child behaved, whether he seemed happy at school and especially how well he got on with the other children and the teacher. Difficulties with discipline or behaviour worried them far more than difficulties with school work. In fact, when asked about his or her performance in school subjects they mostly did not know.

The parents of nearly a fifth of the children in the lowest income did not know about their children's progress at school (see Table 6.1). This tended to be a larger proportion than in the other income groups. When these mothers were asked whether the child was going to the school they wanted them to go to the answer was often, 'Well, its the nearest.' This answer was based on practical considerations for the nearest school involves the least amount of time and

---

4. For a further discussion on the uptake of free school meals see the following Chapter 7, p. 98.

money spent on travelling. A much smaller proportion of the children (10 per cent) in this income group were reported by their mothers to be getting on well at school, compared with 30 per cent of children in the sample as a whole.

TABLE 6.1

Percentage of School Children in Families with Different Incomes, According to Progress at School

Mother's assessment of progress at school	Household Income as a per cent of National Assistance Scale					All School Children
	Under 100	100–119	120–139	140–199	200 and over	
	%	%	%	%	%	%
Good	10	38	26	33	59	30
Average	53	44	55	42	30	46
Bad	18	12	8	16	—	13
Don't know	19	6	11	9	11	11
Total	100	100	100	100	100	100
Number	100	87	89	123	46	445

Some of the working class mothers' concern with their children's behaviour rather than academic progress may have been a reflection of their own anxieties about their abilities in controlling their children, especially those who had reached secondary school. In addition they may have reflected working class attitudes towards the role of education and the difficulties working class children have in adapting to the learning situation at school. Bernstein's study of linguistic development and processes of socialization[5] have revealed important differences between the structure of language spoken in working class families and that which is spoken in middle class families. In working class families the language parents use is much less differentiated, personal and qualified than in middle class families. This restricts the children's ability to express themselves precisely. In addition the use of language in working class families reinforces a passive learning role for the child compared with his counterpart in the middle class family who is encouraged to play an active role.[6] This together with a greater concern for gratification in the immediate rather than the distant future[7] means the working class child has to make bigger adjustments in order to profit from the learning situation at school. 'Thus there is no continuity between

---

5. See Bernstein B., Social Class and Linguistic Development and Theory of Social Learning, *op. cit.*, pp. 290–313.
6. This is discussed fully in Bernstein B and Henderson D., Relevance of Language to Socialization. *Sociology*, Vol. 3, No. 1, January 1969, p. 13. Studies in the use of toys in middle class families and working class families suggest that middle class mothers attach more importance to their educational value than working class mothers. Play has more educational significance for middle class mothers than working class mothers. This is another indication that learning processes in the middle class home encourage an active learning role for the child. This is consistent with the role expected in infant school. Working class children on the other hand have learnt how to utilize the learning opportunities presented to them at school. See Bernstein B., and Young D., Differences in Conceptions of the Use of Toys, *Sociology*, Vol. 1, No. 2, May 1967, pp. 138–139.
7. This has already been discussed in Chapter 5, p. 71 and is also discussed in Chapter 8 on p. 137.

the expectancies of the school and those of the child. In the school an activity or series of activities are meaningful in relation to a distant goal and the present has critical extensions in time and place. The working class child is concerned mainly with the present; *his social structure, unlike that of the middle class child provides little incentive or purposeful support to make the methods and ends of school personally meaningful'* (authors italics).[8] Bernstein's hypothesis that the adjustments to secondary school may be even more difficult than adjustments to primary school because the educational process at this stage increasingly presupposes a culture and socialization the working class child has not acquired[9] was supported by the progress of the children from the poorer large families in this study as reported by their mothers and their teachers. Several (twelve) mothers particularly mentioned that whereas their children had seemed settled and happy at primary school, at secondary school they lost interest and attended irregularly. Also when interviewing the teachers of the secondary school children it was noticed that it was less likely that any one teacher had continuous close contact with any child because of the emphasis on specialist teaching. The lack of a continuous relationship with any one teacher on reaching secondary school can only have added to the insecurity of a child from a home in which he or she received little parental encouragement, and had to share parental attention with several siblings.

The teachers were asked for an evaluation of the children's progress and the head teachers were asked to say whether the child's standard of work had improved, remained constant or deteriorated. No standardized tests were carried out so the following figures are based on individual teachers' assessments. Among the children aged between five and eight years only a fifth (21 per cent of the boys and 23 per cent of the girls) were reading normally. In the next age group (nine to eleven years) the school work of a third (twenty-four) of the children was said to have improved. Ten infant schools and less than half the junior schools were streamed, but among those that were, 11 per cent of the large family children were in the upper stream and 12 per cent in the slow learner streams. In the secondary schools a higher proportion (44 per cent in secondary modern schools and 29 per cent in comprehensive schools) were found in the slow learner streams. The teachers associated deterioration in school work with poor attendance. For example, a third of the secondary school boys were said to be poor attenders and the work of half of them had shown some deterioration. Among the good attenders four-fifths had shown an improvement in their work. Absences were more frequent and lasted longer among the secondary

---

8. Bernstein B., Social Class and Linguistic Development, A Theory of Social Learning, *op. cit.*, p. 307.
9. This is also discussed on p. 91.

school children. Only 40 per cent of secondary school children had not been absent at all from school in the two terms preceding the interview with the mother. Illness was the main reason for absence for all the children (84 per cent of the primary and 73 per cent of the secondary). Both parents and teachers agreed upon this. Other reasons for absence became more important at the secondary school stage, although the teachers emphasized these reasons more than the mothers. Altogether the mothers reported that sixteen children (4 per cent of school children) had been absent from school in the two terms preceding the home interview because their help was needed at home. All but four were secondary school children. The mothers of a further sixteen children reported that they had played truant and again the majority (eleven) were over eleven years old.[10]

The mothers were also asked when they thought their secondary school children would be leaving school. Table 6.2 shows how the mothers in each group answered.

TABLE 6.2

Percentage of Secondary School Children in Families with Different Incomes who were Expected to Leave School at Different Ages

Age at which mother expected child to leave school	Household Income as Per cent of National Assistance Scale							
	Under 100		100 and less than 140		140 and over		All children[1]	
	N	%	N	%	N	%	N	%
15 years	21	(60)	25	44	13	(27)	59	41
16 ,,	7	(20)	13	23	9	(18)	29	21
17 ,,	4	(11)	8	14	9	(18)	21	15
18 or over	3	(9)	11	19	18	(37)	32	23
All ages	35	(100)	57	100	49	(100)	141	100

(1) The total excludes children from families for which income was unknown.

Three-fifths of the secondary school children in the poorest families were expected to leave school at the earliest opportunity. The mothers were not asked directly why they said their children would be leaving at a particular age. However from some of the remarks they made about their children's education it is possible to suggest some of the reasons.

10. From the figures given by the mother, 7 per cent of the secondary school children had played truant within the two terms preceding the home interview and a further 7 per cent had missed school because their help was needed at home. The head teachers, when interviewed, gave higher figures: 21 per cent truancy among secondary school boys and 15 per cent among secondary school girls. Nearly a third (31 per cent) of the girls were reported to have been absent because their help was needed at home. Although these figures are not strictly comparable because they refer to a different period in time (the interviews at the school took place over a year after the home interview and while the mothers were asked specifically about the preceding two terms, the teachers may have been referring to absences over a longer period), the large discrepancy does suggest some of the mothers may have under-reported truancy. The incidence of truancy based on the mothers' figures is not significantly higher than among secondary school children of average or less than average ability. The teachers' figures are much closer to the incidence figures for those in the lower range of ability. A survey made in a sample of modern and comprehensive schools in 1961 found that three per cent of the boys and five per cent of girls in the upper range of ability played truant, compared with fifteen per cent and eighteen per cent of boys and girls respectively in the lower range of ability. Central Advisory Council for Education (England) "*Half Our Future*". H.M.S.O., London, 1963, pp. 199, 203, 219, 223.

For example, there were a few mothers who did not bother much about what happened to their children at school. Like their children they had 'opted out' of the education system. They did not feel that what their children learnt at school was very useful. So what was the point of worrying about what happens at school? When Mrs. Hinton was asked how her fifteen-year-old daughter was getting on at school, she said, 'Linda's leaving in seven weeks. She'll make a good housewife, but she's learnt that at home not at school. She doesn't mind missing school. Like last term she missed a lot. She's got bad circulation so she gets terrible chilblains on her feet— they're so bad she can't walk. The School Board man was ever so nice about it, but I hadn't got doctors' certificates to cover all her absences—I didn't like to keep bothering him—so I was taken to court. They fined me £6 and didn't give me any time to pay so I borrowed it from my sister-in-law. I don't spend much time over schools—though I did go to see Christine's school play at Christmas.' Altogether twenty-four of the school children followed up at school were still at school after the statutory leaving age. Their teachers considered twelve of them to be poor attenders.[11]

Four mothers said they thought the school leaving age should be dropped to fourteen not increased to sixteen. Mrs. Clifford particularly resented keeping her son on at school until he was fifteen, because she felt he would be much more use earning money. 'The school attendance man agrees with me. He says he knows several families where it's stupid to keep the children on, it's such a financial strain for the family. They'd be much better off leaving at fourteen. Of course, it's ridiculous, but when he does leave I'll lose eight bob family allowance and I'll have to pay fifteen bob extra lodger's fee on the rent. They get at you either way don't they.'

Parents with low incomes who did want their children to stay on at school had great difficulties. Even with an education maintenance allowance (maximum grant found in this study was £1 a week) it was hard to continue to clothe their children and their over-crowded homes were not conducive to quiet study and homework. Also the children themselves sometimes felt under pressure to leave at the earliest opportunity. For example, one of the older boys of a

---

11. It is difficult to interpret this finding as it is based on such a small figure and especially as it was found that poor attendance in the upper age groups for all children in some secondary modern schools and streams was common. For example, one class had a 50 per cent attendance in the summer term. The children from large families may, therefore, have been no different from their class mates in this respect, and were behaving as Bernstein predicts lower working class children will when they reach secondary school. 'The character of the educational process changes at the secondary level. It becomes increasingly analytic and relies on the progressive exploitation of what Piaget calls "formal operations" whereas the lower working class child's linguistic history tends to restrict him to the concrete operational stage. This shift of emphasis reveals the inadequacy of the lower working class child's preparation. Although the primary stage is passed without an undue sense of failure or purposelessness, the discrepancy between what he can do and what he is called upon to do widens considerably at the secondary level . . . Failure despite persistence often ensues. Insulation from this failure is accomplished by denying the relevance of education and by the mechanical assertion of his own values. By fourteen years of age many lower working class children have become unteachable.' Bernstein B., Social Class and Linguistic Development. A Theory of Social Learning, *op. cit.*, p. 307.

family of ten in which the father, ill with chronic bronchitis and unable to work regularly, had hoped to stay on at school to take the Certificate in Secondary Education and go on to an engineering apprenticeship. He had been in the 'A' stream at the Comprehensive School he had attended and his teacher said he had a high potential for original work. He had written a 'fantastic' essay on the prices and incomes policy. In addition he had won an award for public speaking and wrote good poetry. His parents had signed for him to stay on until the age of sixteen and they had been told of education maintenance allowances. The head teacher knew the boy would have liked to stay on, however, the boy felt he ought to be helping his family financially so he left when he became fifteen years old and started work as a postman.

The length and standard of education acquired by children from a poor large family was sometimes determined by the low expectations of their teachers rather than by the children or parents. Children from such families sometimes were not expected to do well. An extreme example of this was the second daughter of a family of ten who won a place to grammar school but was later transferred to a secondary modern school. She had not failed to keep up with her school work but her headmaster considered her to be misplaced because she sometimes played truant, and, as he told the interviewer, 'She alone of her family and district came to the grammar school.' In spite of her continued truancy from school she nevertheless managed to stay in the 'A' stream of the secondary modern school.[12]

Altogether fifty-four of the older children from these families had left school by the time their parents were interviewed. The majority (forty-three) had left at the age of fifteen, seven had left at the age of sixteen and only four had had a longer education.

Contacts Between Home and School

We have shown in the previous section that some parents and children did not feel involved in school life. As a result they knew and understood little about the education system. How much contact was there between parents and teachers? How much did the teachers, in their turn know and understand about these children with unusual and, in some instances, difficult home situations.

Unfortunately the mothers were not asked when they last saw

---

12. In a longitudinal study of 5,362 children born in the first week of March 1946, Douglas, Ross and Simpson found that children of large families were more likely to leave school at the earliest opportunity than children of small families. Financial reasons, although important, could not be the sole factor involved for this was true of the *youngest* boys and girls in the families as well as of the oldest. See Douglas J. W. B., Ross J. M. and Simpson H. R. *All Our Future, A Longitudinal Study of Secondary Education.* Peter Davies, London, 1968, p. 128.

Perhaps part of the explanation lies in the expectations of other teachers and parents as well as of the children themselves: they will follow the same educational pattern as that set by the older siblings. In other words the younger children of a large family inherit an educational 'reputation' from their older siblings, which as we have seen, may be poor.

one of the children's teachers and on what occasion this occurred. However, some of the mothers volunteered information about their relationships with their children's teachers and this showed how varied their contacts could be. Mrs. Fuller was one of the few mothers from a family with an income below the National Assistance level who reported frequent contact with the children's school. She used to help with school dinners at her son's school and as a result knew several of the staff well. She often discussed her children's progress at school with the teachers. She visited the school whenever there was a function to which parents were invited and she always felt welcome there. Mrs. Sawyer got on very well with her children's Primary school headmistress and sought her advice on much more than her children's education. 'If I've got anything I don't understand, an official letter or something, I run round and ask her to explain. She's very good and always sorts things out. When your letter came about your survey I went round and showed it to her to ask her what I should do. She said to let you come and see what it was all about—after all I didn't have to answer anything I didn't want.' Mrs. Finsbury's marriage was not a happy one and she had difficulty in managing her ten children, three of whom were attending schools for educationally subnormal children and another a boarding school for maladjusted children. She received a great deal of support from her eleven year old son's teacher. His teacher thought this boy was the most disturbed of all Mrs. Finsbury's children. He often wandered alone at night and was absent from school a third of the time. At school she said that he was very difficult. For example, sometimes he built himself a cave out of boxes in the corner of the classroom and retired into it like a hermit. Every Friday his teacher called on Mrs. Finsbury for a cup of tea and a chat. She made sure the children had the necessary school uniform which had meant taking the boy to the shop as well as getting a grant, because neither parent would spare the time to take him. In addition she gave Michael and his brother half-a-crown pocket money every week. As Mrs. Finsbury said: 'She's a real friend.'

However, not all the mothers had a good relationship with their children's teachers. Mrs. Fielding was particularly bitter because she had had several unhappy experiences. 'My daughter's raincoat was stolen at school. Nearly new it was, so I went to see the headmistress about it. Things are always getting stolen from the cloakroom— goodness knows how many plimsols they've lost—but I can't afford to replace a good raincoat. She said she was sorry and so on but said there wasn't much she could do about it and then turned round and offered me a tatty old raincoat that had been found in the cloakroom and never claimed. I'm not surprised no one wanted it—there wasn't much life left to it. Well if she thought I was going to accept that old thing gratefully she'd got another think coming—I told her she could keep it—that was no replacement for the coat Mary'd lost. I suppose she thought because I had several children and not much money I ought to be grateful for anything she condescended to give me. Oh—you're scarred if you have a large family.' She also felt awkward visiting the school for the same reasons that her children experienced difficulties if they were not wearing a complete school uniform. Lack of money, she felt, put her at a disadvantage because, as she explained, 'If I go to the school for a special occasion—I always try and go to things the children tell me about—I can't dress up and look as smart as some of the other mothers, so the teachers don't bother to come and talk to me.'

Many of these children's teachers' knowledge of their home circumstances appeared to be as sketchy as their parents' knowledge of school life, for there was often little contact with the parents. Over half the secondary school children's head teachers, compared with a third of the primary school children', could not remember when they last saw the parents. The head teacher had more contacts with the parents (usually the mother) in the infants and junior schools than in the secondary schools. The head teachers of a third (fifty-eight) of the primary school children (169) compared with a seventh (fifteen) of the secondary school children (105) followed up at school, had seen the parents of these children during the term in which they were interviewed. This, in spite of the fact, as mentioned earlier, mothers and teachers noticed their children were more difficult at secondary school than at primary school. Many teachers were not happy about this lack of contact and altogether the teachers of two-thirds of the school children thought that their contact with parents was inadequate. Moreover half thought that the school curriculum allowed them too little time to learn of any problem a child might have, and the teachers of only one in five of the schoolchildren thought the school was able to manage a child's social or welfare problems well. There were however a few teachers who felt they should not probe into a child's home life because this was the only way of ensuring the child was treated impartially and one head teacher told the interviewer that it was wrong to inquire about an adolescent's home situation unless the school's involvement was necessary.

Just over a third (105) of the school children were considered by their teachers to have social welfare problems ranging from difficulties with clothing, to stealing or truancy. The extent of these problems was such that ninety-three school children (fifty-six from primary schools and thirty-seven from secondary schools) had been referred to a School Care committee or other welfare agency. When the teachers were asked to say more about the cause of these problems, the majority saw the mother's inability to manage and control the children as the key factors. The teachers of a third (ninety-two) of the children thought their mothers could not manage their problems. Judgements about the mothers' ability to manage her family appeared to be made in many instances without real knowledge of the financial difficulties facing some of these mothers. For example, Mrs. Foster, who had kept her family of eight children on little over £16 for two years since her husband's accident, was described by one of the teachers as 'a poor old thing, who only just coped and that to the level of her ability' without any reference to the financial problems this mother had to overcome daily. In contrast, another mother in similar financial circumstances who had enough energy left to see that her children had the free meals and clothing grants to which they were entitled, was labelled 'a professional sponger who misused poverty'. The head teacher justified this view further by saying that they could afford to go off in the old family van at weekends. He was not aware that the van was run on a lucky football pool win and contributions from the oldest boy who was working. Moreover the family used it to visit a farming friend and bring back fresh vegetables, eggs and occasionally rabbits, which they bought cheaply from him. Another teacher with whom the mother had more contact commented that the children 'looked as fat as butter' adding that he thought she took great care of them.

The teachers of only eighteen children from ten families attributed their problems to an inadequate income alone. Seven of these families had an income below National Assistance level,[13] and the other three an income less than 25 per cent above. In two of these families the teachers of only one child in each family had recognized the financial difficulties of the family. Children from a further four families with incomes below National Assistance level were recognized as having problems. These were not attributed to an inadequate income but were said to result from the mother's inability to care for her children. For example, such children were described as emotionally deprived or lacking parental control. There seems no doubt that the children from the poorest families had difficulties at school, even if the cause was not always recognized by their teachers.

Conclusions

The status of the large family affected every aspect of their lives. In particular it determined the extent to which they felt able to call upon the resources of friends and neighbours. The lives of the parents, particularly the mothers were already restricted because of

---

13. At least one child in sixteen of the eighteen families with an income below National Assistance level were followed up at school.

the time and energy needed to organize a large family. These restrictions were reinforced when there was litttle money by the element of hostility contained in the attitudes of those who worked or lived nearby.

The children of the poorer large families were also at a disadvantage because of their inability to participate in school life to the extent of some of their school mates. They were constantly reminded of their short comings at school, which could have far-reaching effects. The mother's inability to clothe her children as she would have liked or as the school expected did more than place the children in embarrassing and hurtful situations. Research on streaming in primary schools indicates that children who appeared poorly cared for tended to be put into the lower streams. Children who begin in upper streams and move to lower ones tend to be those from large families who received poor care in early schoolhood. 'Streaming by ability reinforces the process of social selection. Children who come from well-kept homes and who are themselves clean, well clothed and shod stand a greater chance of being put in the upper streams than their measured ability would seem to justify. Once there they are likely to stay and to improve in performance in succeeding years. This is in striking contrast to the deterioration noticed in those children of similar initial measured ability who were placed in lower streams.'[14] To a certain extent streaming by ability is streaming by grooming.

It is possible that the educational handicaps of the working class child are magnified by the processes of socialization that occur in a large family. Other research studies[15] have shown that limited contact with parents is likely to reduce the development of a child's verbal abilities. This study did not collect systematic information about the interactions between child and parents or between one child and another in these large families, this would be a major study in itself. The material collected only allows us to suggest that, in all income groups, children received less individual attention from their parents.[16] Moreover lack of parental attention seemed more often to be compensated for by older siblings rather than by other adults (in particular grandparents, aunts or uncles). This may make for differences in the socialization processes to which the child from the large family is exposed, which in turn will affect his ability to profit from the learning processes of school.[17]

---

14. Douglas, J. W. B., Streaming by Ability, *New Society*, February 1964.
15. Nisbet J., Family Environment and Intelligence, *Eugenics Review*, XLV, 1953, pp. 31–42.
16. see Chapter 6, p. 89 and Chapter 8, p. 121.
17. Douglas, Ross and Simpson, noting that the low measured ability of children from large families is probably determined by environmental factors which exert their effect *before* starting school, suggest that 'insufficient attention has been paid to the lack of verbal stimulation that may result when a child, during the years when he is learning to speak spends much of his time with others near his own age'. They then argue that nursery school experience may not compensate for these factors 'unless the proportion of nursery staff is high enough for children to be able to talk and discuss constantly with adults, the already restricted child may suffer further impairment in language development through being thrown into even longer and more intimate association with others of his own age'. Douglas J. W. B., Ross J. M. and Simpson H. R., *op. cit.*, p. 128.

Children from large families are also likely to be further handicapped because it has been found that parental ill-health has an adverse effect on school attainments, particularly when the father's ill-health results in unemployment or death.[18] As we have seen there was a considerable degree of ill-health among the fathers in this study which had prevented the father working.[19]

Their teachers, while nearly always aware that the children from the poorer large families had difficulties, often lacked the time and resources to fully understand them. Their understanding of the stress under which many of the poorer families, particularly the mothers, lived was limited largely because of the lack of communication between themselves and the parents. In addition there was a reluctance to recognize that the incomes on which some families had to live was insufficient for even the most skilled housekeeper to manage. It is probable that the source of this reluctance had much in common with the source of the hostility felt by some of the poorer families in their relationships with neighbours and workmates. Their income level was not far above the total income of these families. They managed without needing extra help because they had been careful not to have more than the average number of children.

---

18 See Douglas J. W. B., Ross J. M. and Simpson H. R. *op. cit.*, p. 94. They found that 'the families of the ill and unemployed are also large: 58 per cent with four or more children compared with 33 per cent in the whole sample'. *Op. cit.*, p. 95.
19. See Chapter 2, p. 29.

To what extent did the social services help the poorer large families? This chapter discusses first the extent to which the families claimed various welfare benefits and secondly the families' relationships with officials from local authority welfare departments, children's departments, and for the poorer families, the National Assistance Board. It should be remembered that the descriptions of these relationships are based only on the families' observations, the officials concerned may well have perceived them differently. However, it is important to know how the families themselves interpreted the policies of the various welfare departments and how they perceived the behaviour of the officials with whom they came in contact. Some families although eligible for assistance in cash or kind to supplement their inadequate money income were not receiving all to which they were entitled. Though the reasons for this were complex, they were often associated with the attitudes of the families themselves both towards receiving assistance and towards those who gave it.

Welfare benefits in Cash and Kind
Free School Meals

One third of the school children entitled to free school meals were not receiving them. Altogether free school meals were received by 104 school children, sixty from famies below the basic National Assistance level and forty-four from families with incomes above this level. There were several reasons for children failing to receive free meals.

In the first place there were children not taking meals at school at all, although in the lowest income group a higher proportion of children took meals—91 per cent as compared with 75 per cent in families with higher incomes. Altogether 60 per cent of the parents of children who would not take school meals said that their children did not like the food provided at school. In some cases this was because they were unused to the wide variety of goods included in school meals. As mentioned in Chapter 3 the poorer children had a very restricted diet at home: their mothers could not afford to buy a wide variety of food nor could they risk wasting food in attempts to persuade a child to eat something new. Moreover some children may not have been able to cope with the mealtime situation, at home they never had a family meal sitting round a table together as there were not enough chairs to sit on.

TABLE 7.1

The Number of Families with Different Incomes who Received Different Welfare Benefits

Education and Welfare Benefits	Household Income as a per cent of National Assistance Scale							All families [1]
	Under 100		100–119		120–139		140 and over	
Free school Meals	17		8		4		1	30
Uniform grants	8	(10)	7	(14)	2	(14)	–	17
Education maintenance allowances	1	(1)	2	(4)	–	(2)	– (10)	3
Extra milk tokens	4	(16)	2		–		–	6
Free welfare food other than milk	3	(16)	–		–		–	3
Clothing from NAB or welfare agency	7		4		–		–	11
Free or subsidized holidays	5		4		5		7	21
All families whether receiving or not receiving benefits	18		15		16		31	80

The figures in brackets are the number of families with dependent children in the age groups to which these benefits apply.
(1) The total excludes six families for whom income was unknown.

In other families pride was a consideration. The stigma attached to receiving free meals has already been mentioned.[1] Altogether four children from families where some children were getting free meals were paying for their meals. Then there was a family of six where all school meals were paid for as a result of the experience of the oldest girl.

Ignorance of entitlement was not a reason for any child missing free school meals. There were no low income families who were

1. See Chapter 6, p. 87.

unaware that the service existed. Either a school care committee worker or a teacher had told them how and where to apply, and having had assurance of their eligibility they had all applied. Two families, however, had applied for free meals and had been refused even though at the time of the interview their incomes were low enough to qualify.[2]

School Uniform Grants

Of the thirty families who were receiving free school meals four had children who were not required to wear uniform and seventeen had had uniform grants in the last year. The uniform grant was not always given in the form of money; instead a voucher was provided to take to a special shop. This carried the implication that the mother could not be trusted with actual cash and would not buy the appropriate items of clothing if given the choice. Rather than ensure wise buying this system meant some mothers had no choice but to buy shirts, blouses, trousers and scarves at what seemed inflated prices. The grants, worth at most £12, did not cover the full cost of the uniform. One mother estimated that it had cost her £21 to buy a complete uniform. A child who had had a uniform grant was not eligible for another two years. When the schools these children attended were visited the head teachers were asked whether they thought these grants were adequate. The head teachers of only sixteen children thought they were adequate, the majority (75 per cent) of head teachers did not know.

Four families had applied for a grant but had either been refused or had received no reply, and a further five families either did not know about them, could not understand how to fill in the form or would not apply because they were proud.

The application form for these grants were far from easy to fill in. As well as requiring many details about their children, evidence of the father's income over the past six months was required. Quite apart from a reluctance to ask an employer to sign the form it was not easy if the father had had more than one job during that period. The self-employed also found it difficult to produce suitable evidence. For example, one mother sent back her application form four times asking what evidence of her husband's income (he was self-employed) was required. Each time her form was returned with no further explanation. In the end she went out and bought the uniform herself. 'He'd have still been sitting at home waiting to go to school if I hadn't, so I went and got it myself. We just went very short for three weeks.'

One father would not fill in a form for a uniform grant, not

---

2. The means test is based on scales similar to those used by the National Assistance Board with an addition of 5s. for each child.

because he could not understand it, and not only because it had to be signed by his employer. He did not want to feel anyone else was supporting his children. They were his children and he was not going to ask anyone for help in looking after them. Altogether a fifth (fifty-four) of the school children followed up at school were thought by their teachers to be poorly dressed.

Good relationships with a teacher or school care committee worker could make an important difference to these families. They were not only better informed about their entitlements but also had someone to help them fill in complicated forms and to make sure they received assistance with the minimum amount of delay. The teachers reported helping thirty-one children to obtain such assistance either with a grant or gifts of clothing. However, over a third (twenty-two) had received no such help from their teachers.[3] Mrs. Fulton was one of the lucky mothers. She had no trouble with uniform grants, and when Tony, her twelve-year-old boy, came home with his blazer badly torn after falling off a fence at school, she had been allowed extra money to replace it without any delay. Mrs. Talbot had not been as fortunate. Once when her son needed shoes it had taken three months from the time she first asked for them until she received them.

Education Maintenance Allowances

These were the rarest grants to be received. Very few families had ever heard of them. Only three children were receiving grants worth on average £1 per week. Only one mother had heard of them, her daughter's headmaster had written to the local Education Department enquiring about a grant for her, two months before the survey. When she was interviewed she had still had no reply. Meanwhile to supplement the family's income she was continuing to work in spite of her doctor's warning that it was bad for her health. Apart from those getting maintenance allowance all the eldest children of the lowest income families either had already left at fifteen or their mothers expected them to.[4] These decisions were made without the knowledge that financial assistance was available for children who stayed on at school.

Welfare Foods

A family with an income at or below National Assistance board scale rates was eligible for free welfare foods and extra milk tokens, worth half a pint per child under five years old. The majority (thirteen) poor families did not know this. As a result only three out of sixteen families with incomes below the National Assistance

---

3. These figures of assistance with clothing are not strictly comparable with those based on the mothers' information as they refer to a period a year later.
4. See Chapter 6, Table 6.2, p. 90.

level and a child of the appropriate age were getting free welfare foods and all of these were actually drawing National Assistance. Only six families had extra milk tokens.

Although seventy-one families had children under five years old, only twenty-one bought welfare foods. Eight said the children preferred sweeter orange juice, ten said the long journey to the clinic was not worth the saving involved. Perhaps if the savings were bigger more would take advantage of welfare foods: after all, the uptake of welfare foods dropped by half in 1961 when the subsidy was removed.

Clothing Grants

There were other clothing grants. Nine families had received a grant for children's shoes in the past year from the National Assistance Board or the local Education Department. Four of the nine families drawing National Assistance had received an exceptional needs grant for clothing during the previous twelve months the largest of these being £12. Altogether, eleven families had been given clothing by a welfare organization.

Families who needed assistance with clothing other than school uniform encountered several difficulties, the major one being the delay in getting assistance. This delay could arise for various reasons. For example, Mrs. Talbot, who was receiving National Assistance because her husband had left her, was uncertain who to ask for help. Once she asked the National Assistance Board for shoes for the two boys. However, she reported that she had been told that they never buy shoes:[5] the school had to buy them because only they could keep an eye on them and know when shoes were needed. Only after Ernest had been kept home from school because he had no shoes to wear was she given a letter to take to the manager of the local Co-op by the school care committee worker. At first he had been reluctant to give them to her because she had not taken Ernest with her so the manager could see he really needed shoes. As she explained, she could not bring him because he had no shoes.

Other families had encountered delay in getting the assistance they needed because they had no one to speak on their behalf. Mrs. Halger, whose husband suffered from chronic bronchitis had been very upset when she had asked for a clothing grant and had been refused on the grounds that she did not need it. 'They said my children always looked alright. Well, I do my best to keep them neat and tidy, and we always try to look our best when we are out, even if we do have to wear old clothes. If I let myself go and didn't

---

5. It has not been past (or present policy) of the National Assistance Board (or Supplementary Benefits Commission) not to give grants for shoes for school children. Whether the source of the misunderstanding was with the local officer or with the mother, the result was delay in assistance reaching the family when they most needed it.

bother they'd have helped me. They don't help those who struggle to keep their self-respect.' The Halger family did not take no for an answer, and contacted the Family Welfare Association who had once given them some toys at Christmas. When they applied to the Board on her behalf she was given £12. Even so, she had been unable to get all the clothes the children needed for the winter including four warm coats. Four would only have been possible if she had bought very cheap, poor quality, and this she knew was false economy. As a result of this experience, she believed that those who did not worry about living off the State and did not bother to manage on what was given them received better treamtent than those who tried hard to manage.

Families without an official to speak for them also ran the risk of being given unsuitable help. For example, the Maclean family were having difficulties with clothing for the children, and Mrs. Maclean had been sent to see the Women's Voluntary Service who had given her some very unsuitable clothes, including a skirt for her ten-year-old daughter that was not only old-fashioned but much too big. Mr. Maclean was very angry and contacted the probation officer he had known as a result of spending a spell in prison. He told him always to get in touch if he ever had any difficulties. The probation officer had talked to the Women's Voluntary Service and when Mr. Maclean went to see them again they had some better quality, more suitable clothes to give him. As he said, 'You have to stand up to them, otherwise they'll give you any old rubbish. It's not that I'm not grateful for help, but take that skirt—it was useless, Linda couldn't have worn it. We couldn't even have remade it because it was pleated and so had faded in stripes. Just because we need a bit of help it doesn't mean we don't care what we look like.'

Holidays

There were also subsidized *holidays*. Education and welfare departments as well as voluntary organizations could help a child to go away for a holiday. Free or substantially subsidized holidays (parents paying less than half the cost) had been provided for seventy children. Twenty-one, a quarter of the families were involved.

As Table 7.2 shows, although nearly a third of the children in the lowest income group had had a holiday in the past year, only 6 per cent (five) of them had spent it with their parents. All the other children had had a free holiday, arranged by the school or a voluntary organization. Holidays with parents were rare except amongst the highest income families. Altogether half the children who had had a holiday had spent it with their parents. Of those who had had a holiday 21 per cent of the primary school children had had a free holiday and 18 per cent had had a subsidized holiday.

Amongst secondary school children a higher proportion had been assisted financially: 32 per cent had had them free and 20 per cent were subsidized. Without this assistance only half the number of children would have been away for a holiday.

TABLE 7.2

Percentage of Children Aged Five and over in Families with Different Incomes who had Subsidized Holidays

Holidays	Household Income as a percentage of National Assistance Scale					All children[1]	
	Under 100	100–119	120–139	140–199	Over 200		
	%	%	%	%	%	%	No.
No holiday	71	63	73	62	(16)	62	236
Free holiday	18	25	3	3	—	10	39
Parents paid half	5	4	8	10	(18)	8	31
Holidays with parents	6	8	16	25	(66)	20	78
Total	100	100	100	100	100	100	384
Number	87	72	80	101	44		

(1) All children excludes children in the six families for whom income was unknown.

Free holidays were not restricted to the poorest families (see Table 7.2). This was because children could be sent away for health reasons. For example, Mrs. Trent's fifteen-year-old son had very bad eczema and asthma and went to Broadstairs for six weeks every spring. 'He gets on lovely in the country—comes back all rosy-cheeked. He's not the same here—London don't seem to suit him.'

Partly subsidized holidays, however, were more frequent in the higher income groups. This was because some of the poorer families could not afford to pay *anything* for a child's holiday[6] and because some schools did not make arrangements for holidays of this kind. Thus whether a child had a holiday or not depended on the initiative of a teacher or social worker.

A free holiday for mothers was much harder to arrange. Only one mother had had a free holiday in the previous year. Altogether eleven of the eighteen mothers in the lowest income group had never had a holiday since they were married.

'Ladies from the Welfare'

There were many different social or welfare workers, both statutory and voluntary, who could become involved in the life of a family with children. For example, every family would have been visited at least once by a health visitor after the birth of a baby, and, if the family situation justified it, she might have been a regular visitor

6. This is an example of the *cost* of utilizing a service preventing its full use, particularly by the poorest families. Roy Parker discusses this and other factors which restrict the use of the social services in Social Administration and Scarcity, *Social Work*, April 1967, pp. 9–14.

until the child goes to school. In London, a School Care committee worker saw any family whom a teacher, for example, thought might be entitled to free school meals. Although it was the head teacher's responsibility to inform parents of uniform grants and education maintenance allowances, a School Care committee worker may have actually investigated the family situation and followed through any application for assistance. Problems of irregular school attendance were investigated by a school attendance officer. A child care officer or probation officer might have become involved with the family if one of the children needed special care perhaps away from home; or if the child had committed an offence. If the family situation was very difficult then a family caseworker might have regularly visited the family on a long term basis. The worker could come from the local authority's Welfare or Children's Department; or from a voluntary organization such as the Family Service Unit or Family Welfare Association. In a crisis the family may have needed a home help. This brought in the Welfare Department. They may have needed money. This could have brought them into contact with the National Assistance Board. As a result of this wide variety of statutory and voluntary workers whom the family could have encountered for one reason or another, they were not always able to attach the correct 'label' to them. So any woman welfare worker could be referred to as 'a lady from the welfare'. How many families had had contact with social workers as well as health visitors? How much assistance did they feel they had received from them?

It was not the poorest families who were necessarily visited the most frequently by a social worker. Eleven of the eighteen families with an income below National Assistance level reported that they rarely saw a health visitor, school care committee worker or any other 'lady from the welfare'. They did not mention any of them as people they would get in touch with when in difficulty.[7]

Although all the families had been visited once by a health visitor and had seen her at the welfare clinic, she was a regular caller on only ten families. Mrs. Leamington liked to feel she called in as a friend. 'Oh, I entertain the health visitor every week. I ask her in, make her welcome and give her a cup of tea. She passes the house, you see, on the way to a clinic.' When in financial difficulties, she asked the health visitor for assistance. In the winter prior to the survey her electricity meter had been broken into and she had either to make up the money or have the electricity cut off. They had no financial resources with which to do the former, so the health visitor had intervened on their behalf and made arrangements to

---

7. This is based on information from the family only. However, even if contact with social workers was under-reported for some reason, these families nevertheless experienced difficulty in obtaining assistance both in cash and in kind.

pay back the money gradually. Nevertheless, their basic financial problem remained untouched by anyone. Mr. Leamington was wage-stopped to the extent of £5 a week at the time of the survey and had been so for three months.

The Bloom family had also received a great deal of assistance from the health visitor. 'She comes as a friend to see me. She doesn't come that often but I can get in touch easily enough. She saw I was very upset about something last time she came so I explained about being behind with the rates and being threatened with the bailiffs. Well she was able to get some money from the L.C.C. Maternity and Child Welfare Fund and they paid it direct to the rating authorities. They'd helped, she said, because it was obvious we were trying to cope.' Another family had been given some toys and extra clothing at Christmas by the health visitor.

Mrs. Clifford however did not want any advice from health visitors because having had nine children she felt she knew more about bringing up children than a woman who had never had any of her own. She resented the young doctor at the clinic for the same reason: practical experience was far better than anything learnt out of books, as far as she was concerned. Only a quarter (twenty-one) of the mothers continued to visit the welfare clinic for long after the baby's birth. If they were worried about the children's health they went to their own general practitioner.

There were few families in regular contact with any other social workers. Four families had had some contact with the Children's Department in the past year because of difficulties with the older children. In three families one of the older children had been caught stealing and it had been thought necessary to take the child into care. For example, Mrs. Leamington's eldest boy had been caught with two other children stealing from the local supermarket. As a result he had been taken into care. A year later he was joined by his younger brother because Mrs. Leamington had felt he was getting beyond her control and so had referred him to the Children's Department herself. A child care officer was visiting Mrs. Wainwright regularly because her son, too, had been taken into care, not only because he stole things both from school and from home but also because of his association with an older man. Mrs. Wainwright found these visits very reassuring, or as she put it: 'She comes as a friend—*not* like the health visitor.'

A further six families had been in touch with the Probation Department in the year prior to the survey. In two families the children had been in trouble for stealing: one had been put on probation and the other taken into care. The latter family had been referred to the Family Service Unit and at the time of the survey was being visited regularly by a family caseworker. Marital problems

106

had brought two families in touch with the Probation service but only for a brief period. The remaining two families had voluntarily remained in contact with a probation officer they had known when in difficulties in the past. Mrs. Walters' first marriage had broken up ten years previously and she and the four children had been turned out into the street by her husband. The probation officer who had helped her through separation and finally divorce had remained in touch with the family. She was godmother to one of the boys and every summer he spent two weeks holiday with her.

Many of the poorer families were reluctant to ask the help of health visitors or 'ladies from the welfare'. Asking for assistance involved them in a considerable loss of pride and self-respect. The families felt that this was not always appreciated by those whose help they sought. For example, when Mrs. Griffin, whose husband had been unable to continue his work as a building labourer during the winter months because of chronic bronchitis, asked the health visitor for a few baby's clothes, although grateful for what she was given resented the health visitor's attitude. 'She asked me if I was really up against it—did I really need them. Well you've got to be pretty desperate to ask for baby clothes. Of course, the baby needed some clothes, I wouldn't have asked else.'

Mrs. Wainwright explained why she needed encouragement to ask for help. Five years previously her husband had had to spend some weeks in hospital suffering from inflammation of the lung and money had become scarce. At that time she pawned her wedding ring for seven shillings and sixpence. At Christmas that year she had asked the Red Cross for a few toys for the children. 'They asked me if I was hard up—was I really on the floor. Now who if they've got any pride asks for second-hand toys for their kids at Christmas. It was the same when the British Legion gave me a pound voucher for groceries, they told me I hadn't to buy any luxuries with it—only necessities. I wouldn't go through the indignities of that again. Still, the last two years have been better. I never ask for grants by myself now—it's only when somebody comes and tells me—then I'll ask.'

Mr. Carstairs, who had two children in care, had asked the Children's Department for clothes, but as he said, 'It's degrading but you have to.' He had been unable to work for three years as he had tuberculosis.

The Experience of National Assistance

At the time of the survey fourteen families were dependent on state benefits. Nine families were long-term recipients of National Insurance benefits together with National Assistance and five were only needing temporary assistance. In the twelve months prior to the survey a further seven families had experienced periods of dependence on National Assistance ranging from one week to three months. Altogether over a third (thirty) of the families had had to rely wholly or partly on National Assistance at some time since their marriage.

Those who had been dependent on National Assistance for some time and were likely to continue to be so because their health was permanently poor or because they were fatherless were less critical of the help they received than those who had only experienced assistance briefly. This was partly because they felt grateful, for, as one father explained: 'After all, I'm placing my large family at the public expense. I get £16 altogether—that's a lot to get for nothing.' Besides the chronic sick had demonstrated that they were 'genuine cases'. Those who needed temporary assistance were more likely to be thought to be 'trying it on' or at least the families thought that this was the attitude towards them. It was also much easier for a family to be critical of an institution on which it no longer depended for its livelihood. Nevertheless, even the long-term recipients of National Assistance were never able to rid themselves of the feeling that they were living off charity. All of them said that they felt as one father who said: 'All right I know I'm entitled to it, but they make you *feel* as if you're begging.'

The experience and feelings of Mr. Manchester when he became permanently dependent on National Assistance show very clearly the shock and the loss in self-respect it had involved for him. He had been discharged from the Army with a severe heart complaint eighteen months before the survey. At first he had lied about his health and taken a job. But he had not been able to keep it for long and had to spent a period in hospital. He had been told he must not do any work that involved physical strain because physical exertion was very dangerous. He had been unable to find suitable work. The doctors had suggested an operation but because the chances of recovery were not very great he had refused. While he was not of much use to his family in his present state of health he was certain that they would be far worse off if he died. Before applying for National Assistance he had used the £320 service grant given him when he left the Army. 'I drew all my savings first—I don't like getting something for nothing, but the school care saw about it—they made me go. I'm the stiff upper lip type—I'd like to manage without help. Now I've not got any private life left, I've forfeited my life by answering so many questions. All my private life is on paper in the National Assistance, the Ministry of Pensions, the Education Department—they've got it several times over. Do you know I had to fill in two separate forms for school uniform for the two girls. It's ridiculous, you'd think they'd only need the details once. I hated going to the National Assistance. I trembled all over in the office.[8] I turned my collar up—I don't know what I'd have done if any of my friends had seen me. There's no privacy there. They have cubicles but they aren't much good—you can still hear what everyone's saying. That's not the end of it—I hate having to cash the allowance at the Post Office. They know I'm on Assistance. On Guy Fawkes I spent a little of it on a few fireworks for the children—the way they looked at me I felt really guilty. It's the same if I buy a book or sweets in the Post Office they make me feel I'm doing something terrible—that I'm wasting their money.' His self-respect had taken a further blow when the school care committee worker, trying to help the family as much as she could, had approached his old regiment for money to pay an outstanding electricity bill. 'She kept asking me for their address so in the end I gave in and gave it to her. I know the money had to come from somewhere but I wish I hadn't. The last thing you do is to go crawling back to your old regiment for help. I can't face her any more—I have to go and sit in the other room when she comes now.' At the time of the survey the family was still failing to keep up with their financial commitments and was £20 behind. Although Mr. Manchester sat down every day and worked out the day's expenditure, he could not allow for the inevitable extras. The family had been receiving National Assistance for seven months then, and during that time had received no extra grants. He refused to ask for anything more than the basic allowance, it was too humiliating. The extreme reluctance of such people to apply for help limited the demands made on the service.

Other families came to terms with their dependence on National Assistance by stressing the distinction between themselves and those who 'took advantage' of it. One man who also suffered from a chronic heart condition never asked for extra grants either because he felt that only those who were 'trying it on' asked for extra. He believed that the National Assistance Board would tell him if he was entitled to anything more than his basic allowance. 'The National Assistance—they're very polite. If you're genuine and have everything above board it's all right. Even so you're begging really, aren't you? A lot do impose when they don't need it, and they're the ones who grumble the most. One bloke spoke to the manager something shocking last week. It's the Post Office who are snooty to me.' Another man went further than this and identified even more closely with widely-held public attitudes. He resented assistance being given to people who would not work. He believed single, able-bodied men under twenty-one should not be able to get National Assistance. As for 'coloured persons'—they did not work and if

---

8. While it was true that he could have been visited in his own home thus avoiding the embarrassment of the office visit, he would still have had to face the Post Office clerks.

they were found work they made themselves disagreeable so that they got the sack and went back to Assistance. He also disapproved of the help given to unmarried mothers. Life should not be made easy for them. National Assistance should not be criticized any more than family allowances, because, he said, 'People should be grateful, they shouldn't criticize. Why should others keep other people's children if they're capable of working. There's plenty of work these days.' He thought that National Assistance officers were 'the finest people in the world—they go out of their way to help you. They lean over backwards to help.' Nevertheless, he had not received or asked for any special grants in the previous twelve months, because 'I do my best to do without'. He had not been informed that the sum he was receiving from the National Assistance Board was £2 16s a week *less* than the total scale allowance plus rent. Registered as a light labourer, and with five dependent children he was subject to the wage-stop.

The two fatherless families were even more sensitive about asking for help. Moreover the mothers needed sympathy and understanding, not just financial assistance. Mrs. Krishnan was Welsh by birth and had married a Pakistani tailor. They had five children. In the year before the survey he had had several periods off work because he was diabetic. Just before Christmas he had left the country to visit his family in Pakistan. It was twenty years since he had been home and Mrs. Krishnan had known he was homesick and wanted to see his mother who was ill. The money for his fare had been collected by the Mosque he attended, but Mrs. Krishnan had known nothing about it until four days before his departure, so she had been very shocked at his going. The family had no financial resources because his earnings in the past year had been constantly interrupted by illness. Mrs. Krishnan approached the National Assistance for help. 'At first they joked and said I'd better go and ask the Mosque for money—they must have plenty of it if they could pay for my husband to fly to Pakistan. I didn't think it was funny—I was very upset at that. In fact, if I'd been a man I'd have hit him. They say things like that and then they wonder why there are fights down there.' At the time of the survey she had no outdoor shoes to wear but she did not like to ask for extra money because she had already had one clothing grant. She said she had been told that she was only allowed one in a year.[9]

Mrs. Talbot had not wanted to go to the National Assistance

---

9. It has not been past (or present) policy for the National Assistance Board (or Supplementary Benefits Commission) to restrict clothing grants to one a year. However scale rates are intended to cover 'normal provision' of clothing and in emphasizing this some officers could have given the families the impression that a clothing grant had to cover a certain period. Misunderstandings of this kind can easily occur over discretionary grants when conditions of entitlement are difficult to assess and difficult to explain to the client. Reports from the families interviewed in this study suggest explanations were rarely attempted, or if they were, were not understood.

Board at all. It had only become necessary when, as a result of taking out a separation order against her husband, she stopped receiving money regularly from him. She had not wanted to take her husband to court because when he left her he sent her £12 a week without rent and whenever she needed extra for the children's shoes or clothes he sent her £15 or £20. After six months she was advised by a solicitor to take out a separation order. 'They said the National Assistance might not be able to help me if he stopped paying unless I'd got a court order.[10] I didn't want to do it, they didn't give me no time to think, I wanted to talk it over but she (the probation officer) didn't ask me anything about what I felt. He was terribly hurt when I took out that separation order—he stopped sending me money regularly. Since then he's appeared in court five times but he won't pay off the arrears. He's supposed to give me £10 a week and the Assistance make it up to £13 7s. When he was in court he produced a wage slip showing he earned £12 5s but I know he works for himself and earns a lot more than that—he's a haulage contractor. I told the Assistance but they said they can't investigate it—"you're on our books, not him, he could sue us for interfering with his private affairs". I was much better off before, and I think he might have come back if I'd not taken him to court—that's what really hurt him.' She felt she had been rushed into taking action which instead of ensuring her security had had the opposite effect. Every week she had to go to court to collect her money. She found this an unpleasant experience and although the National Assistance Board officers who visited her from time to time were polite she always had the feeling she was being 'inspected'. 'Once my uncle was here. He (the National Assistance Board officer) looked at him as if he thought he was my fancy man.' Like many families in receipt of Assistance she was very sensitive to any words or actions that could be interpreted as a criticism of her situation.

The families who had needed National Assistance for brief periods only were much more willing to criticize the Board and the attitudes of the officers they had encountered. Unlike the long-term recipients, they had a lasting impression of having had to demonstrate that they really needed the Board's help. 'A man is undeserving until he proves otherwise,' seemed to them to be the principle upon which the Board gave assistance. There was no doubt this feeling deterred them from applying.

For example, when one man had an accident which kept him from work for three weeks, his wife took on two cleaning jobs rather

---

10. It was not past (or present) policy for the National Assistance Board (or Supplementary Benefits Commission) to make assistance to a deserted mother dependent on the existence of a court order. In this example, however, it was not only the mother who had misunderstood her position but also a solicitor and a probation officer. This had serious repercussions on this family and would suggest that the policy of the National Assistance Board needed to be more widely publicized.

than go to the Assistance Board. Mrs. Saunders lost her purse with the week's housekeeping money in it and went to the Board to borrow some money to tide her over the weekend. 'It's not as if we were asking them to give us money. You'd think we were trying to fleece them. In the end they gave us £4, and yet the coloured man next door to me got £8. It's not right, I wouldn't lower myself to go up there again. I'd rather go without. In fact, I wouldn't send even my worst enemy up there.'

Mrs. Finch resented the procedure for actually getting the money as well as the attitude of some of the officers. 'You go up there and they ask you all those questions, and everyone can hear all your business. Then you go back and sit there like a right Charlie in a line with everyone else waiting to see what you're all going to get. I had to wait four hours once. That's a long time when you've got children at home to worry about. It's the last place you go to when you're up against it.'

Five fathers had needed money from the National Assistance Board when they had to stay at home to look after the children while the mother was ill. Every one of them had experienced great difficulty because the policy of the National Assistance Board was based on the assumption that a man whose wife was temporarily ill would wish to remain at work. The Board therefore, would refer a man in this situation to the Local Authority Welfare Department first, and if alternative arrangements for looking after the family could not be made, then the Board would consider the man's claim to financial assistance. This was reasonable if there were feasible alternatives to a man staying at home to look after the family himself. Clearly this was unlikely for a family with six or seven children some of whom had not started school. Such a family would have needed a full-time home-help and few local authorities had (or have) sufficient home-helps to allow them to give one family so much attention. Even if a home help had been available it would have been a costly arrangement. (The five families who had had a home-help at the birth of the last baby all had an income over £20.) The fathers of the large families in this study resented this policy because it seemed to them that their claim to assistance had to be supported by proof from the Welfare Department and the Children's Department that it would be better for the children and a lot cheaper, to pay them to stay at home. One father was so disgusted at the attitude of the National Assistance Board that he swore he would never go to them again. This policy, while not denying these families financial assistance in the end, also added to their insecurity because of the delay it involved. Mrs. Carter, for instance, was about to go into hospital at the time of the survey to have her eighth child. She had tried to find out if the National Assistance Board would give her husband money while he stayed at home to cope with the children because, having just started a new job after six weeks of illness, he was not entitled to holiday pay. No one would assure her that he would get financial assistance, so in addition to the worry of having a baby which in any case was going to be an extra burden they had not wanted (she had conceived 'during the change'), she had gone into hospital unsure of where money was going to come from to look after the family.

The families themselves distinguished between the 'deserving' and 'undeserving' poor. Having to ask for assistance in the same way and in the same place as those they considered 'layabouts' added to their feelings of degradation. Mr. Bloom, whose experience of redundancy after fifteen years in a steady job had been a great shock, had been very depressed at having to go down to the Labour Exchange and queue for unemployment money like the rest of the people there. The officials both at the Labour Exchange and at the National Assistance Board had been very polite and he had not felt bullied by them, but he was a respectable hard-working person who needed only temporary assistance and, as such, felt he should not have to go through the same procedure as those 'lay-abouts' and 'coloureds' who lived off National Assistance. As his wife explained: 'My husband's really bitter. He'd sooner sweep roads than go to the National Assistance. He couldn't stand it up there. He thinks people on the dole are lazy good-for-nothings. He wouldn't ask for help again.'

Altogether, over a third (eight) families who had experienced National Assistance once, for a brief period only, said they were determined never to ask for their help again. The principle of lesser eligibility, which was self-imposed and reinforced by their interpretation of the attitudes and behaviour of the National Assistance Board towards them, was a strong deterrent against asking for help. As Mr. Manchester said: 'Without a job you've got no status.'

Conclusions

The social services were not playing as important a role in maintaining the poorer families' level of living as existing legislation allowed. More families were eligible for free school meals, uniform and clothing grants and free welfare foods than were actually receiving them. In some instances the children's teachers as well as the families had failed to take the initiative.

First there was lack of information about the help to which the poorer families might have been entitled.[11] In addition, the conditions of entitlement were not publicised and unless they could

---

11. Rosalind Brooke gives further examples of the way in which information is withheld by local authorities in Civic Rights and Social Services. *The Political Quarterly*, Vol. 40, No. 1, January 1969, p. 93.

call upon the support of a teacher or social worker they found it difficult to ascertain them.[12] This did not always ensure that the families knew and obtained their rights, however, for social workers and teachers were sometimes ignorant or uninformed. This was not surprising for information about welfare benefits was often given in a form that was difficult to comprehend. Moreover as we have seen in this and the previous chapter, teachers and social workers often seemed to be only partially aware of the families' financial circumstances. If conditions of entitlement were unclear, then a family ran the risk of being refused assistance. This means that having swallowed their pride and admitting to needing help, they could be told that they were not poor enough, that they should have been able to manage without extra. Discretionary grants, although they allowed for flexibility on the part of those administering them, increased the uncertainty of those applying for them. Families often expected to be told of additional grants and waited in vain, interpreting silence to mean additional help could not be given them.

Second, the results of this study suggest that one of the biggest deterrents to greater use of the social services is that the process for applying for help is unpleasant for the family involved. This unpleasantness does not usually represent an explicit policy, its origins lie deeper in the prevailing values society attaches to 'independence' and 'success' and 'work'. The reported experiences and attitudes of the families in this study demonstrated time and time again that use of the social services, particularly those involving provisions to make up for inadequate earnings, are regarded as a 'last resort'. Families feel they ought to manage without them.[13] When these families had to give evidence of their inadequate incomes in order to prove eligibility for one or other of the welfare benefits, they were admitting to *themselves* as well as to others, that they were poor. In a society that places a high value on an individual being able to maintain himself and his family by his own efforts this is tantamount to admitting that they are failures and that they are unable to manage. This involves a loss of self-respect, which is greatest for those families in which the father cannot work either permanently or temporarily, and so relies entirely on financial support from the State. Although they were grateful for state assistance they also felt guilty and ashamed about accepting it. In an effort to reduce these feelings of

---

12. Rosalind Brooke draws the same conclusion from a survey of people's needs for and use of advice on legal and other welfare matters (The Law and Poverty Survey directed by Professor Abel-Smith and Mr Michael Zander). She writes 'Not only do they need information but the more inarticulate and timid clients of the social services need spokesmen, negotiators and sometimes advocates'. Civic Rights and the Social Services, *op. cit.*, p. 95.

13. Roy Parker argues that similar attitudes exist towards the use of the *personal* social services because of their historical associations with the Poor Law and public assistance and because they were used mainly by those of whom society disapproved or by those unable to use a major service such as health or education without assistance. See Parker, R. A., 'The Future of the Personal Social Services', in *The Political Quarterly*, Vol. 40, No. 1, January 1969, pp. 51–52.

Perhaps the efforts to rid the personal social services of stigma associated with poor-relief, have led to reluctance on the part of social workers to give financial assistance.

guilt and shame the families needed to reassure themselves and others that they had not abandoned society's values towards 'work' and 'independence'. They therefore stressed the difference between themselves and the 'lay-abouts' and 'scroungers' who were also maintained by the State. Although they had experienced social disapproval themselves they were anxious not to be associated with other groups of whom society disapproves and so some families spoke in disparaging terms of unmarried mothers and 'coloureds' who made claims on the State for financial support.

The need of the families to convince themselves and those from whom they sought assistance that they not only needed help but deserved it and were entitled to it effectively limited the demands they made on the community. The families were deterred from seeking assistance as much by the attitudes and values of society which they themselves shared, as by any deliberate policy of those working in the social services.

8. LARGE FAMILIES AND FAMILY PLANNING

The two previous chapters have discussed how members of a large family felt they were regarded by the community in which they lived. This chapter describes the parents' own feelings about having a large family and discusses the extent to which parents had consciously chosen to have more than an average number of children. This tells us something of what the parents thought about having a large family having had one, but little about their attitudes when they were first married. Did their attitudes then diverge from the norm or had their attitudes subsequently been conditioned by the fact of having a large family? Social disapproval of large families took many forms and the families tended to accommodate themselves to this disapproval. Moreover some families had experienced a fall in relative income *after* having children, due usually to loss of a well-paid job after an accident or the onset of ill-health.[1] It seems likely therefore, that their attitudes towards having a large family had changed over time.

The underlying reasons for success or failure in attempts to limit family size are very complex and on the basis of information gained at a single interview with each parent they can only be tentatively explored. Nevertheless the information collected gives some clues as to why some families had exercised a greater degree of control on their fertility than others. Cultural and religious factors appeared to have some effect both on their attitudes towards controlling their fertility and on their ability to do so. However differences in cultural and religious backgrounds do not explain why the parents in this study had behaved differently from the majority of their siblings by having a large family.[2] Is the explanation simply that these parents had married at a younger age and were more fertile than their siblings? If this is so then many of the parents in this

---

1. See Chapter 2, p. 21.
2. See Chapter 5, p. 76.
    Unfortunately information about siblings' age at marriage was not collected. Their siblings however were not all younger siblings of the parents from large families, 16 of the mothers and 23 of the fathers were fifth or later children. Twenty of the mothers and nine of the fathers from large families were first or second children.

study would have had to have exercised greater control over their fertility than is necessary for the majority of couples who want to limit the size of their family. As the following discussion will show the experiences and circumstances of these parents decreased rather than increased their ability to choose the size of their families.

Attitudes to Family Size

For many of the parents, experience of life in a large family was not limited to their present marriage. As shown in table 8.1, nearly half the mothers and the fathers had themselves been brought up in large families. Thus when the parents were asked to say what disadvantages and compensations they felt they and the children gained from being members of a large family some were able to draw on their own childhood experiences as well as their present situation. While the cultural and religious backgrounds of a sizeable minority of the parents may have influenced both their attitude towards and expectations of family life, these factors appeared to have had a greater effect on their attitudes towards birth control as will be seen later in the chapter.

TABLE 8.1

Number and Percentage of Families with Different Incomes whose Parents had had Large Families or were Roman Catholic

Whether mother or father came from large family (5 or more children) or were Roman Catholic	Household Income as per cent of National Assistance Scale							
	Under 100		100 and less than 140		140 and over		All families[1]	
	N	%	N	%	N	%	N	%
One or both parents Roman Catholic	4	(22)	11	(36)	17	(55)	31	37[2]
Mother came from a large family	9	(50)	19	(61)	14	(44)	42	51
Father came from a large family	11	(61)	14	(44)	15	(47)	40	50
All families	18	(100)	31	(100)	31	(100)	80	100

(1) All families excludes six for whom income was unknown.
(2) In all but two couples, both spouses were Roman Catholic.

Altogether twenty-nine couples had been brought up as Roman Catholic. They included fourteen of the eighteen couples who had both come from large families. Seven of the latter group had been born and brought up in Ireland. A total of eighteen couples and one spouse of a further nine couples had come from Ireland, the majority emigrating in late adolescence and coming to London in search of employment.

The Advantages

Companionship was valued most by both the mother and the father. Nearly half the parents among Roman Catholics and non-

117

Catholics alike in all income groups mentioned this as one of the most important advantages of life in a large family. 'There's always something to laugh and joke about. We have tremendous fun sometimes, especially on birthdays and Christmas. Children make a home.' Several parents mentioned the loneliness of only children compared with those who had brothers and sisters. They had noticed how much other children in the street enjoyed playing with their children. 'Our home is always full of children, it seems to attract them like a magnet. Half the street seem to be here sometimes. One little boy even turns up before breakfast to play with ours,' said the mother of ten children. Others remembered their own lonely childhood and were not only determined that their children should not be lonely, but by having several children were providing themselves with the companionship they themselves had missed during their childhood. Mr. Bradford, for example, had been an only child. He had nine children and would like to have more: 'the more the merrier'. When the children were all out of the house he disliked the quiet and loneliness so much that he would go and sit on the seat at the corner of the street just to have people around him. Another father did night work so that he could see more of the children. Altogether seven fathers and four mothers had been only children. Four parents had been brought up in an institution.[3]

TABLE 8.2

Percentage of Parents who Specified the Advantages to the Parents and Children of Being a Member of a Large Family

Advantages of a large family	Advantages to the *children* mentioned by:		Advantages to the *parents* mentioned by:	
	Mother %	Father %	Mother %	Father %
Companionship	56	53	36	41
Security	10	14	12	14
Good character training	24	17	9	7
Intellectual, emotional satisfaction	1	1	11	13
Other	1	7	—	1
None	27	21	33	28
Total	100	100	100	100
Number[(1)]	86	70	86	70

(1) Total number of fathers interviewed was 70.

Closely linked with companionship was the feeling of security engendered by a large family. 'Whatever else they go without they've always got each other,' said one mother. Parents hoped their children would always stick up for each other when they were older, again

---

3. These figures are too small to establish that the numbers brought up in an institution are significantly different from the general population.

sometimes referring to their own experience of having no one to turn to in times of trouble. Others thought in terms of their own security later on. 'I've got eight banks,' said one mother referring to her eight children. 'It stands to reason doesn't it, I've a better chance of being well looked after in my old age because I've got six children,' and 'There's safety in numbers,' were typical of the comments made by the fathers.

The other advantages mentioned differed between income groups. The richer parents were more likely to believe that the experience of living and sharing with several brothers and sisters would teach their children to be less selfish, more tolerant of others and able to mix well, but at the same time teaching them to 'stick up' for themselves.[4] An only child did not have to share either parental attention or toys and other personal possessions and so was likely to be selfish as well as lonely. Over half the mothers and three-quarters of the fathers who mentioned this aspect of large family life came from the top income group compared with only one mother and none of the fathers in the bottom income group. This was not because there was a higher proportion of Roman Catholics in the top income group (see Table 8.1) for altogether eighteen non-Catholics compared with only three Roman Catholics mentioned this aspect. The mothers attached more importance to their children 'having their corners rubbed off' than the fathers. Similarly the belief that the parents of large families were less likely to be selfish than those who had no children was more frequently expressed by the richest parents, especially the mothers. They also felt that the children brought home new ideas which broadened their parents' outlook. On the other hand the richer parents, particularly the mothers, were more aware of the emotional satisfaction they derived from bringing up several children. Seven of the ten mothers who mentioned this were in the top income group.

Altogether over a third (thirty) of the mothers and a quarter of the fathers (twenty) thought there were no advantages to them in having several children. The proportion of mothers in each income group who said this did not vary but among the fathers, only two were in the bottom income group. Fewer mothers and fathers (a quarter and a fifth respectively) thought their children gained nothing from having several brothers and sisters.

These answers suggest that the richer parents, particularly the mothers, were more aware of the effects life in a large family had on the character and emotional development of their children. They

---

4. The same conclusion was reached by James Bossard in his study of large families in the United States of America. 'Large family living makes for an early acceptance of the realities of life. To put it another way, being reared in a large family makes for an early and a continuing adjustment to the changing vicissitudes of a realistic world. Things are always happening in a large family, its members live in an ever changing milieu, minor crises are constantly arising.' Bossard, J., *op. cit.*, p. 310.

were also more willing to admit to feelings of satisfaction in bringing up several children and maybe because financial considerations were not necessarily of paramount importance, their children's future was not dominated by the need to get them earning. They therefore thought of their child's development in much broader terms.

The Disadvantages

Altogether nearly two-thirds of the mothers and fathers thought their children suffered some disadvantage from being a member of a large family. Over three-quarters thought there were disadvantages to the parents. Similar patterns were reflected in the way in which parents talked of the disadvantages of having a large family. Some disadvantages were apparent whatever the level of income, others were mentioned more by one income group than another. Differences between Roman Catholics and non-Catholics were slight.

TABLE 8.3

Percentage of Parents who Specified Disadvantages to Parents and Children of Being a Member of a Large Family

Disadvantages of a large family	Disadvantages to the *children* mentioned by:		Disadvantages to the *parents* mentioned by:	
	Mother %	Father %	Mother %	Father %
Lack of money for food, clothing, and other material possessions	43	46	34	47
Lack of adequate accommodation	8	19	10	16
Lack of time for individual development	9	3	22	16
Extra work	–	–	23	11
None	39	32	17	19
Total	100	100	100	100
Number[1]	86	70	86	70

(1) Total number of fathers interviewed was 70.

Material deprivation was mentioned by equal proportions of parents in each income group. Rich and poor parents alike compared what they and their children had with their friends and neighbours and felt themselves materially worse off. The difference was that the poorer families were constantly reminded of all that they and the children had to go without by other people. In addition, as previous chapters have shown, the money they had available for food and clothing was insufficient to buy adequate amounts of the basic items, let alone the luxury items which the richer parents missed. Consequently some of the poorer families felt guilty about their children's lack of smart clothing, toys and so on. As one mother said, 'I've not been fair on them, having so many. It's the cost of living—you can't bring them up the way you'd like.' However only one mother felt that she and her children were living in poverty. Mrs. Krishnan said bitterly: 'If you want to know what poverty means, come to my house. I've just given up. I feel as if my heart's just flown out of the window and gone away somewhere.'

Awareness of the accommodation problems of a large family were not confined to the lowest income groups, as Chaper 3 showed. The standard and adequacy of the families' accommodation was not related to their income except among the minority who were owner occupiers or private tenants.

The remaining major disadvantages mentioned by the parents showed differences between the attitudes expressed by the mothers and the fathers. A few mothers (eight) and even fewer fathers (two) were worried that the presence of several brothers and sisters did not give each child sufficient time or opportunity to develop in their own way. This, they felt, applied especially to the older children. It has been shown already[5] that lack of space could restrict their activities. In addition younger brothers and sisters inevitably made some demands on their time and attention. To some mothers this was seen as an advantage because it lessened the demands made on them and as one mother said: 'When people ask me how I manage eight children—they have their hands full with two—I tell them that when you have a large family they bring each other up.' However it has the opposite effect on the children, because they can have less parental attention, and this may affect the socializing processes to which the child from a large family is exposed.[6] Some mothers of children with a quiet, reserved temperament realized that some children did not always welcome this degree of involvement with their younger brothers and sisters. One mother explained the oldest son's withdrawn moodiness in terms of a reaction against his younger brothers and sisters who would not let him have the peace and quiet he would have liked. 'He should have been an only child,' she said. Another said that her older children had told her they wished they had been only children.[7]

The lack of opportunity for following their own particular interests was commented on by nearly a quarter (nineteen) of the mothers. Only half as many fathers expressed a desire for more time to themselves, for although it has already been shown that the father of a large family was often very involved in domestic duties, in the majority of families he was away from the home far more than his

---

5. See Chapter 3.
6. See Chapter 6, p. 96.
7. This wish for more attention and time for themselves among the children of a large family may explain why they are less likely to have large families themselves. Bossard notes this in his study of large families of the United States: 'Persons reared in large families do not in turn produce large families. Rather they show relatively many childless marriages and small families'. Bossard, J., *op. cit.*, p. 284.

wife. In addition, four of these fathers were answering in terms of restrictions on their wife's time rather than their own. For example, Mr. Bolton, father of eleven children said: 'I wouldn't have a large family again, it's not fair on the old woman. It means she loses her freedom. It was all right for me, I was in the Navy and away a lot. I've been around and seen things while she's been tied down here. We still hope to go out and about one day when the children have grown up, but she needed a break when they were young.'

Restrictions on their own activities appeared to be noticed more by the richer parents, for half the parents who counted this among the disadvantages were in the top income group. Clearly, their expectations were different, for in fact they had more time than the poorer mothers who did not have any labour saving devices and were more likely to be in paid employment.[8] One reason for this was that a higher proportion (a third) of them had had a longer education than the other mothers,[9] and were therefore more likely to have acquired their own interests. Also, the friends with whom they compared themselves had the time and money to pursue various leisure time activities as well as the inclination to do so. The poorer mothers compared themselves with women who may have had a little more money and time for themselves but for cultural and educational reasons did not expect to follow their own interests outside the home.

Closely associated with aspirations about leisure time activities were expectations about the amount of work the mothers had to do at home. In addition the poorer mothers were so busy that they had little time to stop and think about how hard worked they were. It is not surprising therefore that the richer mothers complained more about the extra work involved in having a large family than the poorer mothers. Half the mothers who mentioned the extra work several children created came from the top income group. Only four came from the bottom income group. The fathers commented on this disadvantage far less than the mothers in each income group (see Table 8.3).

It is hard to conclude on the basis of these answers that the richer parents were more aware of the effect life in a large family was having on themselves and the children because their answers may only have reflected their greater ability to express themselves. However their answers would suggest their expectations about family life were not as limited as those of the poorer parents and that, on the basis of these expectations, they had made, to some degree at least,

---

8. See Chapter 2, p. 20.
9. Altogether of the eighty-six mothers interviewed nearly two-thirds (fifty-five) had left school at the minimum school leaving age but without gaining any qualifications. A further four had taken School Certificate at pass or ordinary level and one at higher level. Only four mothers had received further education after leaving school.

a conscious decision to have a large family. Their answers to the questions about the ideal size for a family would support this hypothesis because it was only among the richer parents that the ideal family was thought to be large.

The ideal family size

As an indication of the number of children the mother would have liked, each was asked whether she hoped her children would also have a large family and what she thought was the ideal number of children to have.

Nearly half (thirty-eight) the mothers thought four children was the ideal size for a family and this proportion neither varied between income groups nor between Roman Catholics and non-Catholics. However, only nine mothers thought the ideal size was larger than this and seven were in the highest income group. Five of these seven were Roman Catholics. None of the poorest families thought the ideal number of children to have was more than four, and half of them thought the ideal number was less than this. In this they were reflecting general social values.

A similar pattern was shown in the mothers' hopes for their children. None of the poorest mothers hoped their children would have a large family. The minority of mothers (nine) hoping their children would follow their example in this respect were nearly all (seven) in the highest income group. Over half (fifty-six) the mothers hoped their children would have a small family.

These answers may have reflected the parents' ideas about the size of family they felt would be socially acceptable rather than their own wishes. If this were so then this is another indication of the differences in the community's attitude towards the large family of the low wage earner and the large family of the professional worker.

The majority of families in this income group therefore were aware that in some respects at least the number of children they had had was not ideal. Only two mothers actually said they wanted to have more children and nearly two-thirds (fifty-five) had, at some time in their marriage used some method of birth control to prevent the birth of further children.

Family Planning

The parents of the large families differed from other couples married between 1940 and 1960 in their use of birth control methods in three important ways: the stage in marriage at which they commenced birth control, the methods they tried and the persistance with which they used them.

Although the majority of the parents had attempted to prevent conception at some stage during their marriage, only one couple admitted to using birth control methods from the beginning of their marriage. This is a very small proportion compared with other couples.[10]

At the time of the survey the majority of the couples had been married at least ten years, half of them over fifteen years. All except one couple were married after 1939 and all except one couple were married before the end of 1957.

TABLE 8.4

Percentage of Parents Marrying at Different Ages

Age at marriage	Mother[1] %	Father[1] %
Under 21	45	12
21 years and under 25 years	35	44
25 years and over	20	44
Total	100	100
Number	84	84
Average age at marriage	21·6	25·1

(1) Excludes two couples from whom age at marriage was not obtained.

As shown in Table 8.4, a large majority of the mothers and over half of the fathers were married before the age of twenty-five years. The age at which they married was below the average for men and women, the difference being greater for those (forty-seven) marrying before 1950.[11] There was little difference between income groups in the proportion of parents marrying before the age of twenty-five years. The proportions of the parents who were married after 1950, when under 25 years of age was not significantly different from the general population marrying between 1950 and 1955. The Roman Catholic couples were nearer the norm for they were a year older on average at the time of marriage than the sample as a whole.

The couples in this survey could be divided into three nearly equal groups on the basis of the success of their attempts to control their fertility. First there were the 'non-users': the thirty-one couples who

10. The Marriage Survey carried out in 1959-60 by the Population Investigation Committee of the London School of Economics interviewed 2,350 ever married men and women, aged between 16 and 59 years in 150 representative parliamentary constituencies. This survey found that 43 per cent of couples marrying between 1940 and 1949, and 45 per cent of couples marrying between 1950 and 1959 had started birth control on marriage. Among sem- and unskilled workers the proportions were 37 per cent and 31 per cent respectively and among non-manual workers 49 per cent and 59 per cent. Pierce, R. M. and Rowntree, G., Birth Control in Britain, Part II. *Population Studies*, XV, No. 2, November 1961. Table 13, p. 141.

11. Average age at marriage during year

	Men	Fathers of large families	Women	Mothers of large families
1939–1950	27·06	24·2	24·75	20·6
1951–1955	26·55	25·5	24·18	22·1

The number of parents of large families was too small to show a significant difference from men and women in the general population, except for the mothers married before 1950. The proportion married before the age of 25 years was significantly different from other women, at the one per cent level. *The Registrar General's Statistical Review of England and Wales for the Year 1960*. Part III. H.M.S.O. London 1962, Table VI, p. 13.

said they had never used any method of birth control other than sterilization. Then there were the 'unsuccessful users': the twenty-eight couples who had tried to limit their fertility at an earlier stage in their marriage, usually before they had become a large family. They had not succeeded and had had on average two more children by the time of the survey. The third group were the 'successful users': the twenty-seven couples who had either decided to limit their families after they had become large or who had used some form of birth control to space their families (only three specifically mentioned this aspect).

TABLE 8.5

*Number and Percentage of Families with Different Incomes
who had Tried Birth Control*

Experience of birth control	Household Income as per cent of the National Assistance Scale							
	less than 100		100 but less than 140		140 and over		All families[1]	
	N	%	N	%	N	%	N	%
None	9	(50)	8	(26)	11	(35)	31	36
Unsuccessful	8	(45)	10	(32)	7	(23)	28	33
Successful	1	(5)	13	(42)	13	(42)	27	31
Total	18	(100)	31	(100)	31	(100)	86	100

(1) All families includes six families whose income was unknown.

A little over a third of the parents of large families had never attempted to use any method of family limitation apart from sterilization. Although at the time of the survey four of these mothers said they intended to visit the Family Planning clinic. The proportion of non-users was the same for those married before 1950 as for those married after 1950. The proportion of non-users in this survey did not differ greatly from that for all couples married during the same period.[12] This finding together with the fact that they had married at a younger age on average, suggests that to some extent family size is a function of fertility and age at marriage.

Half of those in the top and middle income groups, compared with only one couple in the bottom income group, were using some

12. Pierce and Rowntree found that among couples married between 1940 and 1949, and those married between 1950 and 1960, 27 per cent and 30 per cent were 'non-users' when they were interviewed in 1960. They did not enquire directly into contraceptive sterilization and this was not included as a method of birth control. By 1965, when the large families were interviewed these proportions may have decreased; for Pierce and Rowntree found that although the class gradient between those *starting* birth conctrol on marriage persisted, the differences in birth control practice between non-manual and manual groups among those marrying between 1930 and 1949 was no longer significant. The difference lay at the *stage* at which birth control was first practised. They therefore concluded "Some of the 1950's cohort who had only just begun family building, had not yet started to use birth control but were likely to do so later. There is therefore every reason to believe that those recently married informants of whom as many as 70 per cent were already users would eventually adopt birth control to a substantially greater degree than their predecessors". Pierce R. M. and Rowntree G., Birth Control in Great Britain, Part I. *Population Studies, Vol. XV,* No. 1, July 1961, p. 14.

method of birth control at the time of the survey. However as Table 8.5 shows this does not mean that the poorer couples had made considerably fewer attempts to regulate their size. The proportion of couples who had attempted to limit their size (excluding those for whom sterilization was their only way of limiting their fertility) was nearly two-thirds in the top and middle income groups and half in the bottom income group. The poorest couples, however, were less successful at preventing further pregnancies and having failed were less likely to try again. In contrast, none of the couples whose income was over twice the National Assistance level had failed in an attempt to limit the size of their family.

Methods of Birth Control

The methods they used were predominantly those that depended on the initiative of the mother rather than the father. This was a very different pattern from that found among other married couples (see Table 8.6) although the recent introduction of oral contraceptives will have altered this picture considerably in the last five years.[13]

TABLE 8.6

Number and percentages of parents using Birth Control

Methods of birth control	Numbers using at time of survey	Numbers reporting the use at some time		
		Parents of large families		Marriage survey couples married between 1950–60[b]
		N	%	%
Cap	9	22	39	12½
Pill	9	16	28	—
Safe period	9	10	19	16
Sheath	3	10	19	51
Other methods[a]	3	8	14	64
Total	33	55	100	100

(a) 'Other methods' included withdrawal which 17% of couples in the marriage survey using birth control methods had tried, not sleeping together and the use of douches, pessaries, etc.
(b) The pattern for couples married between 1940 and 1949 was very similar. The large families have not been divided into two groups because of small numbers.
Source: Pierce and Rowntree 'Birth Control in Britain, Part II'. *Population Studies* XV, 2, Table 1.

As the Table 8.6 shows the cap had been tried by a much higher proportion of the mothers of large families. This may be partly due to the fact that half of the mothers who had tried to regulate their fertility had received advice from family planning clinics.[14] where the majority of clients at the time when these mothers were first seek-

13. The methods used by parents of large families were significantly different from other couples at the 0·001 level.
14. This is also different from married couples in general. Pierce and Rowntree estimated that of persons married between 1950 and 1960 who had never used any method of birth control only 8·1 per cent received advice from a clinic 11·2 per cent from their doctor. The figure for those married between 1940 and 1949 were 6·3 per cent and 14·9 per cent respectively. Pierce, R. M. and Rowntree, G., Birth Control in Britain, Part II, *Population Studies*, Vol. XV, No. 2, November 1961, Table 8, p. 135.

ing advice were recommended to use the cap.[15] The proportion persisting with the cap however was small and those who failed with the cap were unlikely to try another method. Two went on to use the pill, two had reverted to 'trusting to luck' and the other nine mothers had been sterilized or were waiting to be sterilized at the time of the survey. A higher proportion of couples taking the pill or using the safe period to regulate their fertility had persisted with these methods. The reasons for the parents' failures to limit their fertility can be partly explained by their attitudes towards family planning and towards the particular methods of birth control they had tried.

Attitudes towards Family Planning
The 'Non-User'

'You can't plan a family, marriage would be too cut and dried. Love should be spontaneous. Besides it's a question of conscience. We've been brought up to think certain things are wrong and we try to stick to that. It's not easy for us, not everyone can take the strain of a large family,' said Mrs. Finch, the mother of seven children, explaining why she and her husband had not attempted to limit their family. The feelings of the nine Roman Catholic families and the one Jewish family in this group were similar; they were reluctant to go against their religious convictions. However, six of the nine Roman Catholic families said they hoped the Church would either change its attitude towards methods of birth control, especially oral contraception, or at least give the parents of large families a special dispensation to use them. Only one father, who had had ten children went so far as to say, 'If it's God's will you should have them. After all we're taught that God will provide. We wouldn't use the pill even if the Pope said we could.'

The majority (two-thirds) of non-users had no strong religious reasons for not using birth control. However there was a similar belief among some that it was not for them to decide the number of children they should have. They should not go against 'Nature' or 'Fate' and like the Roman Catholic families they must accept whatever comes. As Mrs. Tully, the mother of nine, said, 'I'm not

---

15. For example, 82 per cent of all clients attending family planning clinics in the Metropolitan area for the first time in November 1960 were advised to use the cap initially, Lafitte, F., The Users of Birth Control Clinics, *Population Studies*, Vol. XVI, No. 1, July 1962, Table 13, p. 26.
   Lafitte comments 'On the whole it seems clinics recommend the cap more or less uniformly to women, regardless of their marital or other personal circumstances. This uniformity could be explained in two different ways. Either it reflects a general consensus among clinic doctors that one contraceptive method, the cap, is preferable to all others, in almost all circumstances or it reflects a general consensus among clinic clients that the cap is the method they wish to try and that one does not normally go to a clinic save to learn about this method. If there is such consensus on the demand side (among clients), it may in turn have been engendered by a previously established consensus on the supply side (among clinic doctors). *Either way the implications are considerable*'. *Op. cit.*, p. 18 (author's italics). Certainly the implications for the families in this survey were important, for so many found the cap difficult to use successfully, and having failed once lacked the confidence to try again.

religious-minded but Nature is Nature. Nature should take its course.' Others felt they *could* not, rather than should not plan their families. There was little point for them to try anything that was not 100 per cent certain to prevent conception because they would be sure to be one of the 'unlucky' ones. Four mothers justified this point of view by giving instances of friends or relatives who had been to the Family Planning clinic and had 'fallen' just the same.

About a quarter (seven) of the mothers in this group said their husbands would not allow them to do anything to prevent conception. Two of them said that they suspected that their husbands thought constant child bearing was one way of keeping them tied to the house. Mrs. Hart explained that the last baby had been conceived at the time she was talking about going out to work: 'It was his fault. He wasn't keen on me going out to work when Stephen started school. So when it came near the time, I fell for this one.' Another mother had been sterilized after her eighth child, but before that had never used any method of birth control. 'The old man believed that having babies kept me tied to the house so that I couldn't go out and about. But I felt like a cabbage sticking indoors all the time. He was dead against me being sterilized for a long time and now he regrets having given his permission. It ought to be the wife's decision only. I'm glad it's all over now, though I feel sad there's no pram around any more. I didn't use anything before and the rhythm method's no good—you can't put a time-table on your urges. (That's if you've any left after having half a dozen children.)' However, a husband who was reluctant to limit his family was not necessarily being deliberately inconsiderate to his wife. For example, the father of fourteen children, explaining why he would not allow the use of contraceptives said, 'I wouldn't use them on my wife—it might do her bodily harm.'

Two fathers who would not contemplate the use of contraceptives said they resented being given advice by other people. 'There's plenty of advice going round if I'd take it. The welfare gave me a booklet but I'm not having them tell me what do do.' There were more parents, however, who said they were too shy to raise the subject of birth control with their doctors or go to a Family Planning clinic, but would have welcomed being told of the possibilities of preventing more pregnancies. Altogether six mothers said they were not interested in birth control. However, seven said they had been too shy to raise the subject with their doctors or go to a clinic and five of them said they were even too shy to discuss sexual matters with their husbands. 'You probably think it odd me having all these kids but I don't enjoy it. I've never discussed anything like that with my husband. I'd be too embarrassed to ask the doctor. It would be different if he suggested talking about it.' The other two had been sterilized just prior to the survey although both would have liked to have done something earlier. 'My husband didn't believe in birth control. I'm sterilized now. I wished I'd asked before, I'd have stopped after the fourth. When I finally did pluck up courage to ask the doctor he said he was so glad I'd asked because the suggestion has to come from me. He couldn't mention it until I did because he said he must not try to persuade me to be sterilized,' said the mother of eight children. The other mother, however, had been sterilized after her eighth child on the suggestion of her doctor.

Altogether eight mothers (three Roman Catholic) in this group had been sterilized by the time of the survey, one mother had arranged to be sterilized shortly. The doctor of two mothers had suggested sterilization but they had not liked the idea. On the other hand two other mothers had asked to be sterilized and had been refused. One of these mothers asked after her ninth child, the other after her fourth. Both had been told there was no need for sterilization as they always had healthy babies.

These couples had had more children than the other couples. Their average size was eight, compared with an average of between six and seven, among those who had attempted to limit their size.[16] Only two mothers in this group actually said they wanted more children because, as one explained: 'I just love babies. That's my trouble.' The feelings of the majority of the other mothers could best be summed up in the words of Mrs. Carter: 'You're always disappointed when you fall for another but you love it when it comes.'

The Unsuccessful Users

The majority of these parents had tried to limit their families before they became large. However, they had not succeeded and by the time of the survey they had had on average two more children since their first attempt.

There were several reasons for the lack of success just over half (twenty-eight) the couples had had when trying to limit their families. Many of them had had to overcome ignorance, shyness and their religious beliefs before attempting to limit their families and then having made the attempt, they had to maintain the struggle against old prejudices and fears. If their first method of birth control let them down, then some were likely to give up altogether. Only six were still using a method of birth control at the time of the survey.

Nearly a third of the couples in this group were Roman Catholic couples. All but two had tried to limit their families before they had had five children and all except two had used methods of birth

---

16. The numbers in each group were too small to establish a statistically significant difference in family size.

control not approved of by their Church. Those couples who had only tried the 'safe-period' both said their last baby had been 'a surprise'. Neither would use any other method of birth control because as one of them explained: 'The essential thing is that the Church ought to get down to it and sanction family planning. But I think that as it isn't sanctioned its a sin to use mechanical means. We've tried the safe period but it hasn't always worked. It's a frustration to have to wait—love is spontaneous—it shouldn't be controlled.' The other mother said she would consider using an oral contraceptive to regulate her monthly cycle but not to prevent ovulation.

The other Roman Catholic couples in this group all believed that the Church's attitude towards birth control should change although few thought a change was imminent. As the father of eight children who had emigrated from Ireland said: 'They hold an outdated view, their rules are too stringent. They're living too much in the past. The choice should rest with the married couple. They'll have to change one day because it's undermining the Faith: lots are leaving the Church because of it. People don't live in tiny villages any more—they're moving around so they can see others do different things. That's what's undermining the Faith. Still I expect it'll take them about a hundred years to change.' Others thought the Church should change not only because it should 'move with the times' but because of the dangers of over-population. They had felt justified in going against the teaching of their Church because, in the words of one mother: 'We reckoned it would be a greater sin to have another child we couldn't feed and clothe properly than to use contraceptives. I hope we don't have any more—it would break my heart.'

Only three of the nine Roman Catholic families were still using the method of birth control they had first attempted. One mother gave up all attempts to limit her family when the first attempt failed and subsequently had five more children. Her attitude was one of resignation. 'You see after the third baby I had very bad legs so the doctor sent me to the Family Planning. They fitted me with a cap but fifteen months later I had the fourth baby. Well after that I fell for babies and had them. I'm not going to take the pill—Nature should take its course.' Altogether three of the Roman Catholic mothers had been sterilized, one was waiting to be sterilized and the other was pregnant at the time of the survey.

Ignorance and embarrassment were the other major barriers to successful family planning. An extreme example was Mrs. Sanderson who had had six children before being sterilized, 'I was really green, I didn't know anything. You see I was brought up in a convent and my father was very strict. When my older sister ran away from home my father became very protective towards me. I was green all right—I didn't know it was possible to have children until you were married. Well, I got married two weeks before the first one was born. Then I had three more before I realized you didn't have to go on having babies one after the other. After that my husband started using things but that didn't work. I'd have gone to the clinic but I had no one to go with, no one to tell me about things. We had two more babies and I was very ill—had haemorrhages with both of them, so when I was pregnant with the seventh, they took it away after four months and then I was sterilized.'

Having surmounted their embarrassment once and asked for help in limiting their families, some mothers were too shy to return to the Family Planning clinic and ask for help a second time. One mother was fitted with a cap after her fifth child: 'I used to use it but I didn't put it in right or something so I fell for Marilyn. I hadn't the courage to go again after falling. I've had five more since then. I was ill for four months after having the twins. The doctors at the hospital say I should be sterilized. I would be if I could. I think I'll have to in the end. I can't keep on can I?' Another had lost the cap and was too shy to return to the clinic. Some mothers stopped using the cap because they didn't like 'messing about' or 'interfering' with their bodies. Others said they could not always afford to buy more supplies and had conceived at that time. Only two blamed their lack of success with the cap on an unco-operative husband, the majority said their husbands were not opposed to their using it. Altogether fifteen of the unsuccessful users had tried the cap as their first method of birth control. Only two of them were still persevering with it at the time of the survey and both were in the top income group. Five went on to try other methods.

Altogether a third of these mothers had tried the pill. However only one mother was still taking it at the time of the survey. Although there was far less embarrassment attached to using it the feeling that they were 'interfering with Nature' remained and this feeling was justified when the pill produced unpleasant side effects. For example one mother rapidly put on three stone in weight after taking the pill, another said it made her 'nervous' so her husband insisted she should give it up, and another had to stop taking it because it produced haemorrhages. Altogether half (eight) of the mothers who had tried the pill had given up because they said it had not suited them. The pill, therefore, is not necessarily the answer to those mothers who have difficulty using the cap.

Lack of success in limiting their families after using some method of birth control had deterred over half (fifteen) of the couples from either persevering with the same method or trying another. Their failure to prevent conception occurred on average a year earlier than those couples who continued practising birth control. They had another child within an average of two years, compared with three years for the latter group. Half of them had conceived again within nine months of the birth of their last child. The poorer couples were the quickest to conceive again in spite of using a birth control method and the most likely to give up after failing once. Eight of the couples who gave up after their first attempt were in the bottom income group, only one was in the top income group. Sterilization appeared to be the only solution offered them and six of the mothers (including three Roman Catholics) had been sterilized and three more were waiting to be sterilized at the time of the survey. However by the time they were given the chance of being sterilized they had had on average three more children since their first attempt at family planning had failed.

The Successful Users

These were couples who had first attempted to limit their families after they had had on average between six and seven children. At the time of the survey they had been successful in preventing further pregnancies for an average of four years. Even if some of these mothers do conceive again before their child-bearing days are over, they can at least be considered more successful than the previous group because they had been able to prevent conception for a longer period of time. The 'unsuccessful' user had only managed to prevent conception for an average of twenty-one months adopting some method of birth control.[17] Only one 'successful' user was in the bottom income group and half were in the top income group. Why had these couples started to practise birth control at a later stage than the other couples and why had they been more successful?

In the first place this group included a higher proportion (half) of Roman Catholic couples than the sample as a whole. This is partly a reflection of the fact that the successful users were found in the top and middle income groups, where there were higher proportions of Roman Catholics (see Table 8.1). It could be argued therefore that the battle between economic necessity and conscience took place at a later stage than for the other couples. However, not all of them were going against their Church's teaching. Five couples were using the safe-period, although as one father said: 'We're lucky, it works for us. I know it's not 100 per cent for everyone.' Two couples were no longer sleeping together. A further five mothers

---

17. Although this seems a large difference, the numbers in each group were too small to establish a statistically significant difference.

were taking the pill, three of them preserving their husband's consciences by not telling them. Only two couples relied on the cap and only one on the sheath.

Most of the Roman Catholic families said they had had a struggle with their consciences whether or not they were using a method of family planning approved by their Church. All but two believed the Church should change its views on methods of birth control, although as one father said: 'It's an awful dilemma—it's hard if they change their mind after we've been brought up to think certain things are wrong and tried to stick to it. It makes you wonder what all the struggle was for—and it has been a struggle.' Mr. and Mrs. Conway had had nine children before they felt justified in going against the Church. 'It was a fight with your conscience the whole time. Roman Catholics have no choice. It's not fair. Now my husband uses things, I can't tell you what a relief it is. I used to be in terror and didn't want to go to bed. I'd sit down here after he'd gone to bed hoping he'd be asleep when I went up. I got in such a state I came out in a rash all due to nervous tension the doctor said. It's a ridiculous situation. I have to confess to the priest that we're using contraceptives and he says he can't absolve me unless I say we won't use them again, so I say we won't. But we both know I don't mean it.' Four of the mothers taking the pill were doing so because their doctor had insisted that they did, pointing out that another child would seriously endanger their lives. Two had been so ill during childbirth the last time that they had been given the last rites. Three of them would have preferred to have been sterilized but their husbands would not give their consent. Mrs. Wainwright on the other hand, had come to terms with her own conscience but had had difficulty in persuading the Family Planning clinic that she had done so. 'They asked me so many questions about my religion, and what would I say to the priest and wouldn't I feel guilty about going against the Church's teaching that they put me off. I wouldn't have gone if I hadn't thought things out first. I went to them for practical advice not a discussion on my conscience.' At the time of the survey she was not sleeping with her husband in order to avoid further pregnancies because she had suffered from thrombosis when she was carrying her last baby.

The other couples in this group had not had to fight their consciences before taking steps to prevent further pregnancies. Only one mother had been unable to tell her husband that she was taking the pill, and another had had difficulty in persuading her husband to let her take it. Half of the fathers in fact said that they were fully in favour of limiting their families. They had taken a more positive part in the decision to limit their families. As one explained, 'It's in my interests after all to be responsible. I'm getting too old to cope with young babies and the sleepless nights and disturbance it involves. I want some peace and quiet. Besides a new baby means more and more of an upheaval for the whole family and you've got to think of the other children, too.'

Only two of these couples were relying on the safe period, as they did not 'fancy' any other method of birth control. Only one couple were not sleeping together and the reasons the father gave for this were rather unusual. 'If you don't want to get a woman pregnant you shouldn't go near her. I don't believe in all these new methods of birth control. Freud was right, unexpressed sexual energy provided the driving force behind man's discoveries and inventions. Without it man's progress will come to an end and man will no longer be self sufficient. That's why I don't approve of birth control.' However, the majority of couples did not have these doubts about birth control. Five were using the cap, three the pill and one the sheath.

The 'successful' users were different from the other couples who had tried to limit their families. They included a higher proportion of Roman Catholics and they were financially better off on average. The methods of birth control they used were different. The 'safe-period' had been found to be a satisfactory method of family limitation for some, and the pill had no unpleasant side effects on those who had tried them. Only a quarter compared with over half of the 'unsuccessful' users had been advised to use the cap. Their own doctors were their major source of advice: only seven had received advice from a Family Planning clinic. In contrast two-thirds of the 'unsuccessful' users had been to a Family Planning clinic. Finally many of the fathers had appeared to take a bigger share of responsibility in the decision not to have any more children, whereas among the unsuccessful users he had played a more neutral role.

Abortion and Sterilization

Both these methods of family limitation were looked upon as a last resort. Nearly a quarter (eighteen) of the mothers said they would have considered having an abortion had they been given the opportunity and their own health or the health of the child would have been endangered if the pregnancy continued. A few mothers felt like Mrs. Carter who had conceived her eighth child during 'the change': 'I wouldn't have minded a 'miss' I'd have been relieved. I think that mothers who have a 'mistake' after their family is complete should be helped. I don't believe in abortion on demand but I think genuine cases should be helped more.' Only one mother had had an abortion and another had been offered one but had refused it. Two more admitted to attempting to get an abortion, one privately and the other from her general practitioner. The former gave up because she could not afford the fee involved and the latter was refused. A further thirty-five mothers said that although they would not contemplate an abortion themselves they were not opposed to others having easier access to abortion provided it was done under proper medical supervision. Some felt anything to prevent an unwanted child was a good thing, while others only approved of abortion in cases where pregnancy was detrimental to the mother's health, pointing out that abortion meant taking a life and this should never be forgotten. Altogether thirty-four mothers were totally opposed to abortion whatever the reason. Sixteen of these mothers were Roman Catholic and justified their attitude with religious reasons. The majority of the rest believed, in the words of one mother: 'If you fall for a baby you should have it.' This attitude to abortion was often consistent with their attitude to birth control in general. Half of the mothers opposed to abortion had never tried to limit their families.

There was far less opposition to the idea of sterilization for the mother. Only sixteen mothers were totally opposed to it. They included thirteen Roman Catholics who were also opposed to abortion. They looked upon sterilization as 'tampering with the will of God'. Nearly half (forty-two) the mothers while not disagreeing with sterilization in principle said they did not like the idea for themselves. 'It's too final' or 'It might make a difference to the marriage' were examples of the reasons given for this attitude.

Altogether sixteen mothers had been sterilized, half of them having tried other methods of birth control first, as discussed earlier. A further twelve said they wanted to be sterilized, five of them having already made arrangements. However the possibility of becoming sterilized usually materialized at a late stage in the development of their family. Eleven of these mothers had had eight or more children. Four mothers had asked to be sterilized before becoming a large family and all had been refused: 'You're not thirty yet— you're too young. You might change your mind and later on want more children. Then you'd blame me for letting you be sterilized' or 'You've only three children, that's not a good enough reason for wanting to be sterilized' were examples of reasons their doctors gave for refusing. One of them later succeeded in being sterilized after her fifth child, 'I had to threaten to put my head in a gas oven before they agreed to it. I wouldn't have done of course, but it was the only way of making them take notice of me,' she said.

Conclusions

The parents of these families had exercised varying degrees of control over their fertility. Some had made no efforts to limit their size. Others, although trying to use some method of birth control after they had had only three or four children, had nevertheless become a large family because of their inability to use a birth control method effectively. The third group appeared more capable of using some method of birth control but did not do so until after they had become a large family, although few had allowed themselves to have as many children as those who had made no attempt to limit their fertility.

However, it was not necessarily true that the parents who had chosen to have large families were those who had either made no attempt to limit their fertility or had only done so after they had had at least five children. As the previous discussion has shown, many of the 'non-users' felt that they were in no position to limit their size and in any case they did not know how. Neither their own doctor nor their husbands tried to dispel their ignorance. In many ways the factors that prevented these couples from even trying to limit their fertility were different only in degree from those that prevented the successful use of birth control methods. Ignorance and embarrassment about sexual matters, both likely to reduce the extent of co-operation between husband and wife, all contributed to these parents' lack of confidence in their ability to plan their families. Religious attitudes appeared to reinforce this lack of confidence and delay the stage at which they first attempted to limit their fertility.[18] However, once they had tried a method of birth control they were likely to persevere and the highest proportion of Roman Catholics was found among the successful users. Half the Roman Catholic couples had used a method of birth control of which their church did not approve.[19] The majority of Roman Catholic mothers, and a slightly lower proportion of fathers believed the Church should change its views on birth control methods.

Lack of confidence in their ability to exercise control over their fertility was a reflection of their attitude to life in general. Lee Rainwater, who has studied the attitudes and success in the family planning among working class couples in the United States.[20] suggests that successful planning depends on two major conditions. The first depends on a person's feelings towards the future: 'An orientation to the future, an ability to look ahead implies that one has some feeling of trust about the future, that one feels the future is in relevant ways reasonably predictable. Implicit in every plan is a belief in a more or less stable world; if one cannot assume a stable predictable world, it is very difficult to plan, since one cannot

18. The Marriage Survey also found that Roman Catholics tended to start birth control later in their marriage. Pierce, R. M. and Rowntree, G., Birth Control in Great Britain, Part II, *op. cit.*, p. 144.
19. The Marriage Survey showed that between a half and a third of the younger generation of Roman Catholics resorted eventually to appliance methods. Pierce, R. M. and Rowntree, G., *ibid.*, p. 144,
20. Rainwater, L., '*And the Poor Get Children. Sex, Contraception and Family Planning in the Working Class*'. Chicago, Quadrangle Books, 1960.

confidentially imagine the conditions being planned for.'[21] The second condition depends on a person's confidence in his ability to exert some control over future events 'Closely related to this (the first condition) is a belief that one can affect one's future, can determine to some extent what will happen. This too, is part of one's hopes about the future. . . . In the real world one must be able to act in specific ways, and acting in these ways requires a certain confidence in one's ability both to control oneself and to be partly in control of the outside world.'[22] Low income couples are much less likely to fulfil these conditions than those with higher incomes. In the first place they have had less education and training, and secondly their experiences are more likely to have convinced them that they have little control over their lives. Many of the poorer large families interviewed in this survey had experienced periods of unemployment and homelessness. Not all the families where the father was in full time employment could be certain of maintaining their household income at a certain level because of their reliance on unpredictable sources of income: overtime and the mother's earnings.[23] As the discussion on housekeeping for a large family has shown, the poorer families had little choice but to live from day to day. Therefore both their past and present experiences militated against making plans for the future. When they did try to exercise some control over their lives by attempting to limit their fertility, failure was regarded as yet another demonstration of the futility of doing anything but passively accepting whatever life had in store for them. Moreover, there was rarely someone to help them find out what went wrong and encourage them to try again. It is hardly surprising therefore that at the time of the survey only one couple in the lowest income group was still using a method of birth control.

Against this must be balanced the feelings of the family, particularly the mother, at the birth of another baby. It could be a great and happy event in spite of, or even because of, the difficult and dreary circumstances in which some of the families live. For once the mother was the centre of attention and the whole family felt a sense of occasion. (One of the reasons some of the mothers gave for preferring to have a baby at home was that then the whole family could participate in the birth.)

The experiences of these couples would suggest that the source of family planning advice as well as the method advised made some difference to the degree of confidence with which they tried to limit their fertility. The least successful mothers who gave up after their

---

21. Rainwater, L., *op. cit.*, p. 51.
22. *Ibid.*, p. 52.
23. See Chapter 2.

first attempt, appeared to be those who were advised to use the cap at a Family Planning clinic. Advice from the family's doctor was more likely to be effective if only because it required less effort to remain in contact. But the doctors appeared to vary greatly in their willingness not only to raise the subject of birth control but to give actual advice. Some mothers would have remained ignorant of the methods by which they could limit their fertility if their own doctors had not taken the initiative and raised the subject with them. Others were not so lucky and had waited in vain for the doctor to start a discussion they were too shy to initiate. Many of the fathers of these large families while not actively opposed to the idea of birth control, did little to encourage their wives to seek advice elsewhere and unlike a large proportion of married men (see Table 8.6) they were reluctant to take the responsibility for birth control on themselves. In these circumstances it is hard to say that the majority of these parents had deliberately chosen to have a large family. Many lacked the necessary information as well as the confidence to plan their families.

9. CONCLUSIONS

There are over a quarter of a million families with five or more dependent children in this country today. This is a study of a small number of them and it is important to remember that these families may not be representative of all large families living in London and are even less likely to be representative of those living elsewhere. Nevertheless this study does illustrate some of the aspects of life in a large family. In doing so important questions are raised not only about the adequacy of methods of adjusting family income to take account of family size but also concerning society's attitudes towards children and the poor.

Since the fieldwork of this study was completed there have been substantial increases in family allowances and changes in other welfare benefits, particularly those affecting families with children. It would be impossible to estimate precisely the effects that these have had on the circumstances of the families in this study without interviewing them again. However it is possible to make a very broad assessment of the impact such changes might make to families with children bearing in mind housing costs, prices and charges for some social welfare provisions have risen meanwhile.

At the time of the survey family allowances were worth eight shillings for the second child and ten shillings for third and subsequent children in a family. These amounts had not changed since 1956. In the autumn of 1967 the allowance for fourth and subsequent children was increased by five shillings and the following April there were further increases so that the allowance was worth fifteen shillings for second children and seventeen shillings for third and subsequent children. Announcing these changes in July 1967, Mr. Gordon-Walker (then Minister of Social Security) estimated that these increases would bring half the poorer families up to the basic Supplementary Benefit level current at the time. In October 1968 all family allowances were increased by three shillings so that at the time of writing they stand at eighteen shillings for the second child and twenty shillings for all subsequent children. This has restored the value of family allowances, relative to average earnings, to almost exactly the same as in 1946, when the total allowance for a three-child family was about 8 per cent of average earnings. It should be remembered that when family allowances were introduced in 1946 they were only about half what Beveridge had recommended based on the subsistence cost of a child. The low initial rate of family allowances (five shillings) was justified by promising free school meals to all school children. This has never been fulfilled and the announcement of the increases in family allowances in July 1967 was accompanied by the news that the price of school meals was to be increased from five shillings to seven shillings and sixpence a week. However, as a concession to large families the fourth and subsequent children in all families irrespective of income were to receive free meals. This together with a publicity campaign to inform families of entitlement to free school meals more than doubled the proportion of school children receiving free meals within a year.[1] The concession to all large families was withdrawn in April 1969, saving an estimated £4 million.

The price of welfare milk has increased to sixpence a pint and the subsidy to local authorities to provide free school milk for secondary school children has been withdrawn. Local authorities still have the option to continue to provide free milk by paying for it out of the rates, but at the time of writing none were doing so. Welfare milk and school milk made an important contribution to the diet of some of the poorer families in this study. Milk from these sources accounted for one third of their total milk consumption. Any measures to reduce the supply of cheap or free milk to children are likely, therefore, to have a detrimental effect on the diets of the children of poor, large families.

Income tax allowances for children have not increased since this study was carried out, neither have income taxpayers benefited fully from the recent increases in family allowances because the cost of the increase was largely offset by 'adjusting' the child tax allowance. Parents paying income tax at the standard rate pay back in extra tax nearly all of the increase in family allowances and those paying back at the lower rates, a smaller part of the increase.

Not all recipients of State benefits have benefited to the full extent of the increase in family allowances because dependency benefits in social insurance and social assistance schemes were not raised in line with the increase in family allowances in April 1968 although the smaller increase in October 1968 was reflected in increases in Supplementary Benefit rates. Families who were subject to the 'wage-stop' have, however, benefited fully from the increases

---

1. Statistics of Department of Education and Science. (Personal communication.)
     The children of families receiving supplementary benefit or living at an equivalent standard are entitled to free school meals.

in family allowances because family allowances are a component of their 'normal income'.

Since this study was conducted average earnings have increased. Between January 1966 and January 1969 average earnings of all employees have risen by 20.1 per cent.[2] Prices have not risen quite as fast and in February 1969 they were 15 per cent higher than the monthly average for 1965.[3] There has been, therefore, on average, an increase in real incomes since the beginning of 1966. However, there are still a considerable number of men earning well below the average. A survey of the distribution of earnings of a random half per cent of employees carried out by the Department of Employment and Productivity in September 1968 found that 7.9 per cent of adult male employees working full time were earning a gross weekly wage or salary of £15 or less.[4] There are therefore approximately 900,000 adult males in full time employment earning £15 a week or less. At current Supplementary Benefit level rates these men have a total net disposable income marginally below basic Supplementary Benefit level if they have five children,[5] assuming that the children are receiving free school meals and welfare milk, and that they are benefiting from a rate rebate and rent rebate (based on the model scheme recommended by the Ministry of Housing and Local Government and assuming a rent of £2 a week plus rates of £30 a year). The same survey found that 1.4 per cent (approximately 200,000) of adult males working full time were earning a gross wage or salary of £12. Making the same assumptions these men will be below the basic Supplementary Benefit level if they have only two children. If they have a large family they will be considerably below this level. The problems arising from low wages have not therefore substantially altered since the fieldwork of this study was conducted although the recent increases in family allowances have improved the position of the low wage earner with several children.

The parents in this study came from all social classes so not all of them had a low or inadequate income. One of the aims of this study was to find out the nature of the restrictions their unusual size imposed on their daily lives and to what extent these restrictions were made worse by a low income and modified, or even removed, by a high income. In addition we wanted to know how much support these families, especially the poorer families, received from the social services as well as from friends and relatives. Was this support readily forthcoming and sufficient to alleviate some of the problems facing these families or was it lacking because, as

2. Central Statistics Office, *Monthly Digest of Statistics*, London, H.M.S.O., March 1969, p. 132.
3. *Ibid.*, p. 134.
4. *Department of Employment and Productivity Gazette*, London, H.M.S.O., May 1969, p. 407.
5. The number of men with five children is probably small for 20 per cent of men earning less than £15 a week were under age 25 and 23 per cent were over 60, either of these categories being likely to have five (dependent) children. *Department of Employment and Productivity Gazette, op. cit.*, Table 8.

members of a minority group, they were regarded with disfavour by the community at large? Finally, we wanted to explore the parents' own attitudes towards having more than the average number of children.

The majority of the families have several sources of income. Their standard of living is determined not only by the total amount of income they receive but also by the reliability of each source of income. The level below which the family's income cannot fall depends on the father's basic wage or salary together with family allowances. However basic wages are low for the majority of these fathers. Children's tax allowances adjust family income to family size to a limited extent and affect the rich families more than the poorer ones. Family allowances, although they have doubled in size since this study was carried out, are still too small to cover the subsistence cost of a child as William Beveridge originally intended, so although important to a large family, they do not ensure that the family income is adequate. In these circumstances overtime earnings together with mother's earnings become the major methods by which the family's income is brought up to an adequate level. Other research has shown that fathers of large families work longer hours on average and that the lower his earnings the more likely the mother has paid employment. However it is also found that these methods of supplementing the family's income are likely to be unreliable, especially for the large family. The fathers as well as the mothers experience more interruptions in work. The father's ill health is the main cause for these interruptions. In addition there are times when the father's ill health, while not preventing work altogether reduces his capacity to work long hours. In the twelve months prior to the survey illness had affected the earning capacity of one in four of the fathers. Seven of these fathers were chronically ill and were unlikely to work again and eight had illnesses of a recurrent nature. By the time that family building has been completed the parents tend to be in their forties, and at the stage when the needs of the family may be greatest, when the children are aged from, say, five to fifteen years, the father may be in his fifties. By this time most men have passed the peak in their earnings and are more prone to illness.

The amount of money some families receive from the Supplementary Benefits Commission (the National Assistance Board at the time of the study) to supplement unemployment or sickness benefit is limited by the operation of the 'wage-stop'.[6] 'Normal earnings' are hard to assess when a man's earnings fluctuate, so they are likely to be assessed on the stable element of a man's earnings—basic

---

6. The 'wage-stop' is only applied to short-term (i.e. less than three months) sickness benefit recipients.

wages. These together with family allowances determine the maximum amount of money the family receive from the state in the form of National Assistance. Thus although in theory, state benefits take family size into account by giving an allowance for each child in the family, the extent to which these allowances in practice adjust the income of the low wage earner with several children during periods of sickness or unemployment is limited. Ten of the fourteen families in this study who were dependent on state benefits did not receive the National Assistance scale allowances in full because of the operation of the 'wage stop'.

A low income places severe restrictions on the lives of some of these families. These restrictions are felt in many aspects of their lives. Choice of accommodation is restricted because these families need more rooms than the average house or flat. The richest families in the study had been able to buy large enough houses with all the amenities they needed. As their families grew in size they had been able either to build extensions to the house in which they were living or to move to a bigger one. The families with less money to spend on their accommodation and no security on which to raise a mortgage had to rent their accommodation. The fact that a significantly higher proportion (three-quarters) of large families than households in general are living in rented accommodation at the time of the survey suggests that large families have less chance of buying their own homes than smaller families. This would not matter if they could find adequate rented accommodation, but the experiences of these families indicate that in London at least, rented accommodation which is suitable to the needs of these families is in limited supply. This is true of the private market and of local authority housing. As a result the majority of large families have no choice but to live in overcrowded flats or houses, many of which lack the basic amenities.

A low family income places restrictions on all members of the family but in many ways it is the mother who feels them most. Firstly, the mothers economize most severely on expenditure on themselves. Although the diets of all members of the poorer families are restricted compared with the higher income families, it is the mother who is the most likely to go without cooked meals completely. All members of the poorer families rely to some extent on second hand clothing, but the mothers are often dressed entirely in second-hand clothing. Eleven of the poorer mothers had not bought a new coat or dress since their marriage. In the winter when fuel is precious these mothers work in a cold home all day, saving the fuel for the evenings when all the family is at home. Secondly, the mothers in the low income families almost invariably have complete charge of the family's finances, because their housekeeping is done on a day

143

to day basis. The mothers in these families are dependent on other sources of income besides the father's earnings. These essential supplements to the housekeeping money—family allowances, their own earnings and working children's contributions, are given directly to her and so are under her control. As the housekeeper she, more than any other member of the family, is responsible for keeping a tight control over the family budget at all times. The poorer mother has no alternative but to buy 'little and often' or resort to buying on credit. They know these are expensive methods of buying, but they have insufficient money to practise economies of scale. Even daily budgeting does not enable some families to stretch their income over a full week so they have to borrow money regularly. Three quarters of the families below basic National Assistance scales were in debt at the time of the survey. In contrast, the richer parents are able to share their responsibilities for managing and running the home more than the poorer parents. They are able to budget over a longer period of time and while the mothers are responsible for daily or weekly payments, the fathers are responsible for making long term payments. Over half those with incomes over 40 per cent above this level had savings.

In one respect however, the responsibilities of the poorer parents are shared to a greater extent than among richer families, because there are more occasions when their roles are interchanged. The mother sometimes has to act as partial breadwinner by taking paid employment when the father's earning capacity is reduced and the father has to take over the role of housekeeper when other members of the family are ill. Not only are these occasions more likely to occur in the poorer families but they have little outside help to call upon at these times. Lack of time and money make it more difficult to maintain contacts with relatives from whom they are physically isolated. (Three quarters of the parents in this survey were no longer living in the same London borough or town in which they were born, a third came from outside London.) Only the richer families can afford to take advantage of improvements in communications and so maintain mutually helpful relationships with relatives who live elsewhere. The poorer families are also more reluctant to call upon the help of neighbours, partly because they do not want to accept help they feel unable to return and partly because relationships with neighbours are sometimes strained. These families therefore have little choice but to see themselves as a self-sufficient unit seeking support from each other but not from 'outsiders'.

Where the father of a large family has a high and reliable income the lives of both parents and children reflect few of the restrictions felt by the poorer families. However, family size imposes certain patterns of organization on the family, irrespective of income.

Cramped accommodation lacking in amenities add considerably to the amount of energy needed to run a large household while washing machines, automatic dish washers and other labour saving devices remove much of the drudgery from the housework of those families able to afford them. However there is a limit to the amount of time even the richest families can save because of the amount of time and attention the children seek from their parents is difficult to reduce. The richer parents felt restricted compared with their friends who have fewer children, because their continual involvement with the children leaves them little time to have their leisure activities together. On the other hand they want more time to spend with each of their children individually. In some families the responsibilities are divided between the mother and the father, the mother being more concerned with the younger children and the father with the older ones. Nevertheless the amount of attention each child receives from their parents is limited because of the demands of the siblings. The organization of a large family is therefore likely to have considerable implications for the patterns of socialization of children brought up in a large family, particularly if lack of parental attention is compensated for by attention of older siblings rather than other adults. Many of the parents in this study stressed the value of learning to share and co-operate with other members of the family. Others were aware that there was less opportunity for the children to develop their own interests. We need to know far more about these aspects of large family life and at the same time we need to know to what extent the socialization processes that occur in large families in all income groups determine these children's intellectual development. The material collected in this study only allows us to suggest that given the nature and structure of the education system, children from large families are likely to be at a disadvantage compared with children from smaller families and although material deprivation magnifies these disadvantages it is not their sole cause. Many teachers while recognizing these children, particularly from the poorer large family, are likely to be at a disadvantage compared with children from smaller families, lack the time and resources to fully understand and deal with these problems.

The results of this study demonstrate that the methods of adjusting family money income to family size are unsatisfactory, particularly for the poorer families. Methods of supplementing low wages are either inadequate like family allowances, or unreliable like overtime earnings. When the father is out of work, the inadequacies of low basic wages and family allowances are perpetuated by means of the 'wage stop'. These inadequacies are likely to remain as long as family allowances fail to be seen as an integral part of any incomes policy and as long as they are considered apart from the regular reviews of dependancy allowances in social insurance, social assistance and income tax.

A family's low income can also be supplemented by welfare benefits in cash and kind. These too fall short of meeting the needs of the poorer families. One reason for this is that the benefits are basically too low. For example, there are rent rebate and differential rent schemes which take no account of household size and are based solely on total household income. Consequently in this study the majority of the low income families were found to be in rent arrears.

A second and more important reason lies in their administration. The experiences of the families in this study illustrate the importance of ensuring that the methods by which welfare benefits are administered are known and understood by those who need them. Misunderstandings about the conditions of entitlement to assistance can result in families making the wrong decision which could have a long term effect on their future welfare. For example, in this study there was a mother with eight children who had been deserted by her husband. Mistakenly she had the impression that she would be entitled to receive help from the National Assistance Board only if she took out a court order against her husband. This action not only probably diminished the chances of a reconciliation but also reduced the amount of financial support the father was prepared to give. Families who are not told of benefits to which they may be entitled conclude, often wrongly, that assistance is not available to them. Those who are well-informed and persistent are more likely to receive the benefits to which they are entitled but they run the risk of being labelled 'scroungers'. The support of a social worker or teacher often increases a family's chance of receiving benefits because it reassures the family that they are entitled to assistance and because it helps to convince officials that the family 'deserves' it. The families who receive all the benefits to which they are entitled are not necessarily the poorest. Other families are ignorant of the availability of the assistance they clearly need. They are not in contact with anyone able to dispel their ignorance. The experiences of the families in this study show that sometimes social workers and teachers have insufficient information about the family's financial circumstances as well as about the conditions of entitlement, to enable them to help a family receive as much assistance as existing provisions allow.

The third reason is a more fundamental one. Society has ambivalent attitudes towards those who need support, particularly financial support from the State. On the one hand we believe everybody has a right to financial security in times of adversity and dependancy in childhood, sickness and old age. People have a right to work and those who are unable to do so should be given financial assistance. The State therefore makes provisions to assist people during these periods. On the other hand we still place a high value on independence. Success is measured by a man's ability to support himself and his family by his own efforts. Financial security is a reward for hard work and so must be earned. Those who have to ask for assistance in feeding and clothing their families feel a loss of self-respect and status because it means admitting to themselves as well as to others that they have failed. The methods by which some of the benefits are administered : the means test procedures and the distinction made between the recipients of these benefits and those who can afford to pay (as for example, children receiving free school meals were identified by the other children in their class) reinforce these feelings and make the families concerned feel that perhaps they do not deserve such help. Vouchers instead of money to buy a school uniform for example, carry the implication that unlike the majority of people the families cannot be trusted to spend money wisely. These methods of administration are the consequence of selective services argues Richard Titmuss: 'Universality in welfare is needed to resolve and remove barriers of social and economic discrimination. Separate services for second class citizens invariably become second class services whether they are organized for 10 per cent or 50 per cent of the population. Moreover, those who staff the services may come to believe that they themselves are second class workers. Hence when exercising discretionary powers in giving or withholding benefits and services they may adopt a more punishing attitude to those whom they may disapprove of.'[7]

The further we move away from universal services available as of right to everyone by virtue of citizenship, towards selective services concentrating on 'the poor' the greater the sense of stigma attached to using the services. 'Those who use the minority public services come to feel that they represent a "public burden"; they cannot respect themselves nor do they respect others for using a public service. The implication then is that they can only achieve self-respect (and avoid shame) by not using a public service, by going without, by living in poverty, by not bothering anyone, by retaining their independence or by attempting to buy in the private market.'[8] It is therefore, the implicit values society places on 'work', 'success' and 'independence' which effectively restrict demands on the social services. The families in this study shared these values and therefore restrained their claims for welfare benefits just as much as those who administered them. As a result the inadequate incomes

7. Titmuss R. M., Goals of Today's Welfare State in *Towards Socialism*, edited by Anderson P. and Blackburn R. for the New Left Review, Fontana Library, London, 1965, p. 357.
8. Titmuss R. M.,The Right to Social Security, *Unequal Rights* Child Poverty Action Group and London Co-operative Society Education Department, London 1968, p. 9.

of some families are not supplemented although the State has made provision to do so.

The lives of the parents and children of large families are affected by their status within the community. Society tends to disapprove of those who fail to, or choose not to, limit their fertility unless they are prosperous. The richer families therefore suffer no loss of status because their several children are not seen to increase their dependence on the State. The poorer families do feel a loss in status, especially if the father is sick or unemployed. A low income clearly reduces the level of material comfort of a large family to that well below the standards set by the rest of the community. Their low status magnifies their feelings of deprivation and serves to increase their isolation from relatives and neighbours as well as from the social services. Ironically, inability to control their family size, whether for religious reasons, ignorance or failure of techniques, perpetuates and increases the lack of control and choice in all other aspects of their lives. It is essential therefore, that parents rich or poor should be given adequate help to limit their fertility if they want to do so. The Family Planning advice and assistance some of them, particularly the poorer parents, had received had not been sufficient or of the right kind to enable half of those parents who had attempted to limit their fertility to do so successfully. This is not to suggest that the problems of the poor large family could, or should be solved by ensuring that low paid workers only have one or two children but that the ability to choose the number of children they have should be as great for poorer parents as for richer parents. This choice will not be a real one if children from poor large families continue to experience the deprivations and the restricted opportunities of many of the poorer children in this study. Over twenty-five years ago Eleanor Rathbone, one of the chief advocates of family allowances for *all* children, irrespective of the father's income, said: 'Children should receive a little share of the national income given to them not in respect of their father's service in industry but *in respect of their own value to the community as its future citizens and workers*'[9] (author's italics). The responsibility is ours if we allow large families such a small share of the community's resources that their children can only become second-class citizens and workers.

---

9. Eleanor Rathbone speaking in the first debate on family allowances in the House of Commons, June 1942. Hansard, Vol. 380, col 1866

The Sampling Procedure

The Ministry agreed to use their family allowance records to obtain a sample of 150 families to whom they were paying four or more family allowances. Records for England and Wales are kept at Newcastle. They are in chronological order and are not arranged by area or region. It is reasonable to assume therefore, that the names are in random order. Names from the records were extracted until there was a total of 150 large families living within the London postal district. (To confine the sample to a smaller area within London would have made the sampling procedure considerably longer.) The sample was intended to give, as near as possible, the same number of families with five, six and seven children and rather fewer eight-child families.

For reasons of confidentiality the Ministry did not disclose the names of the families drawn from the records before contacting each family themselves. They therefore wrote to each family in the sample enclosing a letter from us explaining the purpose of the survey. The letter began:

'Dear Madam,

We are research workers from the University of London who are trying to study the financial problems of people who have large families, like yourselves. When we know the facts we hope to write a book because we feel that people do not know enough about the special problems of bringing up a large family and how you manage. Of course we shall not mention any names, and nothing you tell us will be passed on to any Ministry or to the tax authorities.'

Then followed instructions as to how to reply. With this letter each family received a stamped postcard on which the Ministry had printed the name and address of the family, with a request that any family interested should post it back to us, after which I would call and explain the survey.

The Survey Response

Distribution by size of families in sample compared with distribution by size of families receiving family allowances at 31st December 1964

(excluding families with less than five children)

	Number of children				
	5	6	7	8 or more	Total
Families receiving allowances on 31/12/64					
Number (thousands)	134·4	55·8	22·7	14·6	227·5
Per cent	59	25	10	6	100
Original sample					
Number	41	45	46	18	150
Per cent	27	30	31	12	100
Families interviewed					
Number	18	23	30	15	86
Per cent	21	26	35	18	100
Sampling fraction (response) per 1000	0·14	0·38	1·10	1·03	

Letters were sent in January 1965, to which we received thirty-five replies. In the Autumn of that year the Ministry agreed to send a reminder letter. Fifteen families had moved since the sample was drawn (nearly a year had elapsed) and so were not contacted. Thirty-eight families informed the Ministry that they did not wish to take part in this study at this stage and a further ten told me when I called on them that they did not wish to be interviewed—not always because they were not interested or resented 'snoopers', but because they were too busy. The remaining fifty-two families were successfully interviewed. Several said they were glad to have the opportunity of being included in the survey after all. They had intended to reply to the first letter but had not done so because the postcard had been forgotten, lost or destroyed by the children. Others explained that the first letter arrived in the middle of a family crisis and had been overlooked for that reason. The experience with this sample confirms the finding that postal sampling, however carefully the letters explain the purpose of the survey is likely to produce a poor response. A personal explanation together with assurances that questions that offend or worry them, need not be answered, is much more likely to dispel misunderstanding and mis-apprehension about the nature and purpose of the survey. This procedure almost invariably brought co-operation.

Differential response rate

The characteristics of the families who responded to the first letter were different in some respects from those included in the survey at the second stage. The thirty-five families interviewed in the spring 1965 included all five families in Social Class I, five of the seven families in social class II and six of the twelve families in social class V. Among social classes III and IV only a minority of those who were eventually interviewed responded to the first letter: fifteen of the forty-one families from social class III and four of the twenty-one families from social class IV. The median incomes of the two groups were very close although the first group included seven of the twelve families with a weekly income over £35. Most of the very large families were included at the second stage for only five of the seventeen families with at least nine surviving children were interviewed in the Spring 1965 together with half of the families with eight or fewer surviving children. This would suggest that lack of time was one reason for not replying to the first letter.

The total response rate varied directly with size of family. Those with five dependent children having the lowest response rate (41 per cent) and those with eight or more dependent children the highest (80 per cent). Part of the explanation for this difference might be that those who have only five children are less likely to consider themselves to be a 'large family' and declined to take part for that reason. (A few of the five-child families who were interviewed remarked that they were surprised to be included in a study of 'large families'.) The mean number of surviving children born in these families was seven, the mean number of dependent children in the families at the time of the survey was six. The bias towards the very large family, introduced at the sampling stage was therefore increased by these differential response rates.

Three objective measures of the large families' housing have been used:

1. the amount of space per person
2. the condition and amenities of the house
3. the surroundings of the house

1. *Household space*

   There are three different standards by which a household's requirements of space are measured and by which overcrowding is defined.

   (a) The first is the *statutory overcrowding standard* which was introduced in the Housing Act 1935 and has not been changed since. Rooms are allocated as follows: Children under 10 years are counted as half a unit and those under a year are not counted at all. Persons over 10 years can share a room only with someone of the same sex, unless they are man and wife. All rooms including the living room can be used for sleeping in and only if a room is smaller than 110 square feet is the number of permitted persons reduced. This standard has not been used because as the Milner Holland report states[1] 'In some circumstances the statutory standard permits a certain degree of overcrowding.' This seems to apply particularly for large families. For example the standard would allow a husband, wife, six children under ten and twins under a year old only three rooms.

   (b) *The bedroom standard.* This is a more sophisticated and generous version of (a) although it is by no means luxurious. No allowance is made for a spare room, teenagers may have to share with young children and all rooms except the kitchen can be slept in. It is assumed that all rooms can be shared however small. The rooms are allocated as follows: Each married couple given one room and any other person over 21

---

1. Housing in Greater London (The Milner Holland Report) *op. cit.* p. 81.

years is given one room. Children under 10 years old can be paired and can share a room with either sex and persons over 10 years may only be paired with persons of the same sex.

(c) *Ratio of persons per room.* This is a very simple measure of overcrowding and the one used by the Census. Each person in the household is counted as one regardless of age, and the number of persons per room in the dwelling, is calculated. If there are more than $1\frac{1}{2}$ persons per room then the household is considered to be overcrowded. (This is more generous than the statutory overcrowding standard which is roughly equivalent to 2 persons per room. In practice for large families it is equivalent to the bedroom standard *plus* either one extra room or a kitchen large enough to eat in, neither of which are used for sleeping in.)

2. *The conditions and amenities of the house*

There are official standards by which the structure, state of repair and amenities of a house can be measured. A useful and acceptable standard is that used for administering the system of discretionary improvement grants payable under the Housing (Financial Provisions) Act 1958. This is often referred to as the '*12 point standard*', and it provides that a dwelling must:

(a) be in a good state of repair and substantially free from damp;

(b) have each room properly lighted and ventilated;

(c) have an adequate supply of wholesome water laid on inside the dwelling;

(d) be provided with efficient and adequate means of supplying hot water for domestic purposes;

(e) have an internal water closet, if practicable, otherwise a readily accessible outside water closet;

(f) have a fixed bath or shower in a bathroom;

(g) be provided with a sink or sinks, and with suitable arrangements for the disposal of waste water;

(h) have a proper draining system;

(i) be provided in each room with adequate points for gas or electric lighting (where reasonably available):

(j) be provided with adequate facilities for heating;

(k) have satisfactory facilities for storing, preparing and cooking food;
and

(l) have proper provision for storing fuel (where required). The standard used by local authorities to determine if houses are fit for habitation i.e. the *minimum fitness standard* takes the following into account :

(i)   repair;
(ii)   stability;
(iii) freedom from damp;
(iv)   natural lighting;
(v)   ventilation;
(vi)   water supply;
(vii) drainage and sanitary conveniences;
(viii) facilities for storage, preparation and cooking of food and for the disposal of waste water.

Both these standards were used in the following way. Each item on the 12-point scale was given a score of 0, 1 or 2 points. A score of 1 was given if the amenity was present but unsatisfactory: for example a bath with no hot water tap. Each dwelling therefore could have a maximum score of 24 points and any score below this indicated that the dwelling was unsatisfactory, although only if the score is below 23 points has the dwelling been classified as 'poor housing' because some households may only have scored one on an item of relative unimportance (e.g. fuel storage space).

The minimum fitness standard has been applied more strictly in that any house which does not score full marks on the relevant items has been classified as unfit to live in.

3. *The surroundings of the house*
This is an additional measure and at present has no official status except in the form of recommendations by the Dennington Committee which was set up in February 1965 to examine minimum tolerable standards of housing accommodation. This committee felt that more emphasis should be placed on the effect of unsatisfactory environment on housing conditions.

Detailed information about noise, fumes, etc. was not collected as this was beyond the scope of the questionnaire. Instead three factors taking into account the position of the dwelling and its surroundings have been used. These factors affect particularly the family with several children: playing space, facilities for washing and drying clothes, the position of the dwelling if in a block of flats without a lift.